the HIDDEN LIFE *of* PRAYER

AND

the PRAYER-LIFE *of* OUR LORD

the HIDDEN LIFE *of* PRAYER

AND

the PRAYER-LIFE *of* OUR LORD

DAVID M. M'INTYRE

GRANTED
MINISTRIES
— PRESS —

HANNIBAL, MISSOURI
WWW.GRANTEDMINISTRIES.ORG

The Hidden Life of Prayer and The Prayer-Life of our Lord
David M'Intyre, D.D.

Copyright © 2012 by Granted Ministries Press.
Published by Granted Ministries Press, *A Division of Granted Ministries.*

Interior Layout by Jerry Dorris, Authorsupport.com. Cover Design by Scott Schaller.
Cover Painting by Rebekah Gates.

For information or additional copies of *The Hidden Life of Prayer and The Prayer-Life of our Lord* and other resources write:

Granted Ministries Press
120 North Third Street
Hannibal, MO 63401 USA

www.grantedministries.org
orders@grantedministries.org

Library of Congress Control Number: 2011938785

ISBN 978-0-9840318-1-8

Printed in the United States of America

2012

TABLE OF CONTENTS

the HIDDEN LIFE *of* PRAYER

the PRAYER-LIFE *of* OUR LORD

PUBLISHER'S PREFACE

The book you now hold in your hands will perhaps prove to be one of the most helpful devotional classics ever put together on the subject of prayer. David M. M'Intyre has given us two book-length treatments on the topic. The first, The Hidden Life of Prayer, is already widely considered one of the greatest and most helpful books on the subject ever written. It should be read thoughtfully and carefully. Christians from all over the world have reaped great benefits from its contents.

The second, The Prayer-Life of Our Lord, is not as well-known, but it is no less helpful to the Christian yearning to grow strong in the privilege and discipline of prayer. Upon seeing the Lord Jesus Christ in prayer, the disciples earnestly requested he teach them to pray as he did, such was the kind of freedom, reverence and fellowship he had with the Father. It was M'Intyre's belief that Christians can still benefit from meditating on those marvelous and awesome meetings between the heavenly Father and incarnate Son. We should be simultaneously *led to worship* and *challenged to follow* our great Savior. Taken together, the present volume should provide such stimulus to the soul as to warrant repeated readings over the length of one's Christian pilgrimage. We are deeply indebted to our brother for these books.

As a publisher we have changed precious little, fixing a few typos and altering punctuation where necessary to make the reading a little easier for the average reader. We trust the contents of the material will be of tremendous blessing to the body of Christ.

May the Lord help us to "pray always and not lose heart."

– **C.T.** *December, 2011*

the HIDDEN LIFE *of* PRAYER

But thou, when thou prayest, enter into thine inner chamber,
and having shut thy door, pray to thy Father which is in secret,
and thy Father which seeth in secret shall recompense thee.

–Matt. 6:6

AUTHOR'S PREFACE TO SECOND EDITION

The occasion* which has prompted the dedication of this book permits me to inscribe upon it the honoured name of Dr. Andrew A. Bonar, and to recall the fervent devotion which characterised those who were most intimately associated with him in the service of Christ.

The Diary of Dr. Bonar, already a Christian classic, is probably the best treatise on private prayer which we possess. Originally meant to mark the memorabilia of his life, it became, almost exclusively, an instrument for recording and testing his prayers.

On Thursday, 4th December, 1856, Mr. Bonar was inducted into the pastoral charge of Finnieston Church, Glasgow. On the evening of that day he signified anew his sense of the value of prayer: "The Lord filled me with desire, and made me feel that I must be as much with him alone as with souls in public."

A few months later he wrote: "For nearly ten days past have been much hindered in prayer, and feel my strength weakened thereby. I must at once return, through the Lord's strength, to not less than three hours a day spent in prayer and meditation upon the Word."

On the first anniversary this entry occurs: "Tomorrow I propose to spend the most of the day in prayer in the Church. Lord, help me." Later, we find him setting apart one whole day in each month for prayer and fasting. But his devotion overflowed all prepared channels. Sentences such as these carry with them their own instruction: "Felt in the evening most bitter grief over the apathy of the district. They are perishing! They are perishing! And yet they will not consider. I lay awake thinking over it, and crying to the Lord in broken groans."

Again, he observes, "I should count the days, not by what I have of new

---

* The Jubilee of the Finnieston Church, Glasgow, of which Dr. Andrew Bonar was Minister. Dr. M'Intyre was colleague and successor to Dr. Bonar and also son-in-law.

instances of usefulness, but by the times I have been enabled to pray in faith, and to take hold upon God." At another time he remarks that "Prayer should make room for itself"; again, that it should "interweave" itself into all work for Christ; again, that in "the incessant occupations, the bustle of even right things, Satan may find his opportunity to hinder prayer." He quotes Flavel: "The devil is aware that one hour of close fellowship, of hearty converse with God in prayer, is able to pull down what he hath been contriving and building many a year"; and he adds from his own experience, "Satan, like the lapwing, drew me away from the real object (prayer and fellowship with God) by suggesting every now and then something about some other part of my work...and so the best hours of yesterday were in great measure lost, so far as 'prayer and transfiguration' might have been."

His holidays were especially opportunities of "trading with the talent of prayer." "I see," he writes, "that the Master teaches the necessity of such times of continued waiting on God as a stay in the country presents." In sailing to America to attend the Northfield Conference, and in returning, he was "enabled to pray some hours every day in the ship." Of his frequent visits to Mull, he writes, "The best thing I have found in this quiet island has been seasons of prayer."

And as he reviewed his ministry from time to time, amid many regrets his deepest sorrow was on account of the unexhausted possibilities of prayer: "My heart smites me still for being unlike Epaphras, who 'laboured fervently in prayers.' " "One terrible failure confronted me everywhere, viz.: 'Ye have asked nothing in my name.' " "Want of prayer in the right measure and manner." "Had some almost overwhelming sense of sins of omission in the days past. If I had only prayed more." "Oh, that I had prayed a hundred-fold more."

Perhaps the most intimate of Dr. Bonar's ministerial associates was Robert Murray McCheyne. His prayerfulness has almost become a proverb. Dr. James Hamilton writes of him:

He gave himself to prayer. Like his blessed Master he often rose up a great while before it was day, and spend the time in singing psalms and hymns and the devotional reading of that Word which dwelt so richly in him. His walks and rides and journeys were sanctified by prayer.... There was nothing which he liked so much as to go out into a solitary place, and pray; and the ruined chapel of Invergowrie, and many other sequestered spots around Dundee, were the much-loved resorts where he had often enjoyed sweet communion with God. Seldom have we known one so specific and yet reverential in his prayers, nor one whose confessions of sin united such self-loathing with such filial love. And now that "Moses my servant is dead," perhaps the heaviest loss to his brethren, his people, and the land, is the loss of his intercessions.

Only a few months before his death, Mr. McCheyne drew up some considerations touching *Reformation in Secret Prayer*. "I ought," he says, "to spend the best hours of the day in communion with God. It is my noblest and most fruitful employment, and is not to be thrust into any corner." This paper on personal reformation is evidently left unfinished. "And now," adds his biographer, "he knows even as he is known."

Dr. Moody Stuart was a friend greatly beloved. Of him his biographer writes: "Dr. Moody Stuart was preeminently a man of prayer.... He prayed without ceasing.... He prayed always with all prayer and supplication in the Spirit, watching thereunto with all perseverance. He felt that nothing was too small for him to bring to his God in prayer, and that nothing was too great for him to ask in Jesus' name.... Prayer was to him a second nature." His own testimony was, "I cannot say that a day passes without beholding the beauty of the Lord, and being revived by his grace. For the most part the Lord is with me the greater part of the day, and is daily giving me some new insight into the depth and freeness of his love, together with the conviction of sin and contrition of spirit, in which there is much peace and rest."

The rules which he offered to others, and in accordance with which he guided his own prayer-life, were: (a) Pray till you pray; (b) Pray till you are conscious of being heard; (c) Pray till you receive an answer.

Dr. A. N. Somerville was another "true yoke-fellow." In the work of his own congregation, it was his custom "to go into the church alone, and go over the pews, and, reading the names of the sitters in them commit them to God in prayer." When the missionary hunger seized and held his heart, he used to spread open before him an atlas, and pray for men of every nation and kindred and people and tongue. And from the chair of the General Assembly of his Church he exhorted her members to address themselves to more fervent and believing intercession: "The greatest, the most successful servants that Christ ever had divided their functions into departments – 'We will give ourselves continually to prayer and to the ministry of the Word.' What would be thought of dividing the twelve hours of our day by giving six hours to prayer for the Gospel and six to the ministry of the Word? Had all Christ's servants acted thus, could anyone estimate how mighty the results on the world would be today?"

Of William C. Burns, another fellow-soldier, it is said, "His whole life was literally a life of prayer, and his whole ministry a series of battles fought at the mercy-seat." Very early in his ministerial course he gave it as his judgment that "The great, fundamental error, as far as I can see, in the economy of the Christian life, which many, and alas! I for one commit, is that of having too *few* and too *short* periods of solemn retirement with our gracious Father and his adorable Son, Jesus Christ." From this opinion he never swerved. He spent days and sometimes nights "before the Lord," and sighed, "Oh, for a day every week to spend entirely in the secret of his presence." For weeks before the Kilsyth awakening, as his brother informs us, "he was full of prayer; he seemed to care for nothing but to pray. In the daytime, alone, or with others, it was his chief delight, and in the night watches he might be heard praying aloud." And the Lord whom he sought came to his temple *suddenly.*

One might speak of John Milne of Perth, Patrick Miller of Dundee, Daniel Cormick of Kirriemuir, Dr. Bonar's brothers, Dr. James Hamilton of London, Joseph Wilson of Abernyte, and the rest, their "friends and companions." Let it suffice to mention only one other, William Hewitson of Dirleton. Dr. Andrew Bonar says of him, "One thing often struck me in Mr. Hewitson. He seemed to have no intervals in communion with God – no gaps. I used to feel, when with him, that it was being with one who was a vine *watered every moment*." And so it was that he was able to say in truth, "I am better acquainted with Jesus than with any friend I have on earth."

Books on secret prayer are without number; but it seems to me that there is still room for one in which an appeal may be taken, steadily, and from every point, to life – to the experience of God's saints. In these pages no attempt has been made to explain the mysteries of intercourse with God and commerce with heaven. What is here offered is a simple enumeration of some things which the Lord's remembrancers have found to be helpful in the practice of prayer. The great Bengel explained that if he desired the most perfect intimacy with real Christians on one account rather than another, it was "for the sake of learning how they manage in secret to keep up their communion with God."

Lord, teach us to pray.

My God, Thy creature answers Thee.
–Alfred de Musset

The love of Christ is my prayer-book.
–Gerhard Tersteegen

Prayer is the key of heaven;
the Spirit helps faith to turn this key.
–Thomas Watson

CHAPTER 1

The Life of Prayer

1. INTRODUCTION

In one of the cathedrals of Northern Europe, an exquisite group in high relief represents the prayer life. It is disposed in three panels. The first of these reminds us of the apostolic precept, "Pray without ceasing" (1 Thess. 5:17). We see the front of a spacious temple which opens on the market-place. The great square is strewn with crowds of eager men, gesticulating, bargaining—all evidently intent on gain. But One, who wears a circlet of thorn, and is clothed in a garment woven without seam from the top throughout (John 19:23), moves silently through the clamorous crowds and subdues to holy fear the most covetous heart.

The second panel displays the precincts of the temple and serves to illustrate the common worship of the Church. White-robed ministers hasten here and there. They carry oil for the lamp, water for the laver, and blood from the altar; with pure intention, their eyes turned toward the unseen glory, they fulfill the duties of their sacred calling.

The third panel introduces us to the inner sanctuary. A solitary worshipper has entered within the veil and, hushed and lowly in the presence of God, bends before the glancing Shekinah. This represents the hidden life of prayer of which the Master spoke in the familiar words, "But thou, when thou prayest, enter into thine inner chamber, and having shut thy door, pray to thy Father which is in secret, and thy Father which seeth in secret shall recompense thee" (Matt. 6:6 RV).

Our Lord takes it for granted that His people will pray. And indeed in Scripture generally the outward obligation of prayer is implied rather than asserted. Moved by a divinely-implanted instinct, our natures cry out for God, for the living God. And however this instinct may be crushed by sin, it awakes to power in the consciousness of redemption.

Theologians of all schools, and Christians of every type, agree in their recognition of this principle of the new life. Chrysostom has said, "The just man does not desist from praying until he ceases to be just"; and Augustine, "He that loveth little prayeth little, and he that loveth much prayeth much"; and Richard Hooker, "Prayer is the first thing wherewith a righteous life beginneth, and the last wherewith it doth end"; and Père la Combe, "He who has a pure heart will never cease to pray, and he who will be constant in prayer shall know what it is to have a pure heart"; and Bunyan, "If thou art not a praying person, thou art not a Christian"; and Richard Baxter, "Prayer is the breath of the new creature"; and George Herbert, "Prayer … the soul's blood."

2. Prayer is Hard Work

And yet, instinctive as is our dependence upon God, no duty is more earnestly impressed upon us in Scripture than the duty of continual communion with Him. The main reason for this unceasing insistence is the arduousness of prayer. In its nature, it is a laborious undertaking, and in our endeavor to maintain the spirit of prayer we are called to wrestle against principalities and powers of darkness (Eph. 6:12).

"Dear Christian reader," says Jacob Boehme, "to pray aright is right earnest work." Prayer is the most sublime energy of which the spirit of man is capable.[1] It is in one aspect glory and blessedness; in another, it is toil and travail, battle and agony. Uplifted hands grow tremulous long before the field is won; straining sinews and panting breath proclaim the exhaustion of the "heavenly footman." The weight that falls upon an aching heart fills the brow with anguish, even when the midnight air is chill. Prayer is the uplift of the earth-bound soul into the heaven, the entrance of the purified spirit into the holiest, the rending of the luminous veil that shuts in, as behind curtains, the glory of God. It is the vision of things unseen, the recognition of the mind of the Spirit, the effort to frame words which man may not utter. "A man that truly prays one prayer," says Bunyan, "shall after that never be able to express with his mouth or pen the unutterable desires, sense, affection, and longing that went to God in that prayer." The saints of the Jewish Church had a princely energy in intercession: "Battering the gates of heaven with storms of prayer," they took the kingdom of heaven by violence (Matt. 11:12). The first Christians proved in the wilderness, in the dungeon, in the arena, and at the stake the truth of their Master's words, "He shall have whatsoever he saith" (Mark 11:23). Their souls ascended to God in supplication as the flame of the altar mounts heavenward. The Talmudists affirm that in the divine life four things call for fortitude; of these, prayer is one. One who met Tersteegen at Kronenberg remarked, "It seemed to me as if he had gone straight into heaven, and had lost himself in God; but often when he had done praying he was as white as the wall." David Brainerd notes that on one occasion, when he found his soul "exceedingly enlarged" in supplication, he was "in such anguish, and pleaded with so much earnestness and importunity," that when he rose from his knees he felt "extremely weak and overcome." "I could scarcely walk straight," he goes on to say, and "my joints were loosed, the sweat ran down my face and body, and nature seemed as if it would dissolve." A living writer has reminded us of John Foster, who used to spend long nights in

---

1. "Believe me, to pray with all your heart and strength, with the reason and the will, to believe vividly that God will listen to your voice through Christ, and verily do the thing He pleaseth thereupon—this is the last, the greatest achievement of the Christian's warfare upon earth. *Teach* us to pray, O Lord." –Samuel Taylor Coleridge

his chapel, absorbed in spiritual exercises, pacing to and fro in the disquietude of his spirit, until his restless feet had worn a little track in the aisle.[2]

One might easily multiply examples, but there is no need to go beyond Scripture to find either precept or example to impress us with the arduousness of that prayer which prevails. Should not the supplication of the Psalmist, "Quicken Thou me, according to Thy word . . . quicken me in Thy righteousness . . . quicken me after Thy loving-kindness . . . quicken me according to Thy judgments . . . quicken me, O Lord, for Thy name's sake" (Ps. 119), and the complaint of the Evangelical Prophet, "There is none that calleth upon Thy name, that stirreth up himself to take hold of Thee" (Isa. 64:7), find an echo in our experience? Do we know what it is to "labour," to "wrestle," to "agonize" in prayer?[3]

Another explanation of the arduousness of prayer lies in the fact that we are spiritually hindered: there is "the noise of archers in the places of drawing water" (Judg. 5:11). St. Paul assures us that we shall have to maintain our prayer energy "against the rulers of the darkness of this world, against spiritual wickedness in high places" (Eph. 6:12). Dr. Andrew Bonar used to say that, as the King of Syria commanded his captains to fight neither with small nor great, but only with the King of Israel (1 Kings 22:31), so the prince of the power of the air (Eph. 2:2) seems to bend all the force of his attack against the spirit of prayer. If he should prove victorious there, he has won the day. Sometimes we are conscious of a satanic impulse directed immediately against the life of prayer in our souls; sometimes we are led into "dry" and wilderness experiences, and the face of God grows dark above us; sometimes, when we strive most earnestly to bring every thought and imagination under obedience to Christ, we seem to be given over

---

2. Dr. Horton, *Verbum Dei*, 214.

3. "It is a tremendously hard thing to pray aright. Yea, it is verily the science of all sciences even to pray so that the heart may approach unto God with all gracious confidence, and say, 'Our Father, which art in heaven.' For he who can take to himself such confidence of grace is already over the hill of difficulty, and has laid the foundation-stone of the temple of prayer." –Martin Luther, *Parting Words* (Edin., 1903), 73. "Perfect prayer is not attained by the use of many words, but through deep desire." –Catherine of Sienna

to disorder and unrest; sometimes the inbred slothfulness of our nature lends itself to the evil one as an instrument by which he may turn our minds back from the exercise of prayer. Because of all these things, therefore, we must be diligent and resolved, watching as a sentry who remembers that the lives of men are lying at the hazard of his wakefulness, resourcefulness, and courage.[4] "And what I say unto you," said the Lord to His disciples, "I say unto all, Watch!" (Mark 13:37).

3. We Must Be on Guard

There are times when even the soldiers of Christ become heedless of their trust, and no longer guard with vigilance the gift of prayer. Should any one who reads these pages be conscious of loss of power in intercession, lack of joy in communion, hardness and impenitence in confession, "Remember from whence thou art fallen, and repent, and do the first works" (Rev. 2:5).[5]

> O stars of heaven that fade and flame,
>> O whispering waves below!
> Was earth, or heaven, or I the same,
>> A year, a year ago!
> The stars have kept their home on high,
>> the waves their wonted flow;
> The love is lost that once was I,
>> A year, a year ago.[6]

---

4. "We know the utility of prayer from the efforts of the wicked spirits to distract us during the Divine office; and we experience the fruit of prayer in the defeat of our enemies." – John Climacus, *The Holy Ladder of Perfection*, 28.64. "When we go to God by prayer, the devil knows we go to fetch strength against him, and therefore he opposeth us all he can." –Richard Sibbes, *Divine Meditations*, 164.

5. "If thou find a weariness in this duty, suspect thyself, purge and refine thy heart from the love of all sin, and endeavor to put it into a heavenly and spiritual frame; and then thou wilt find this no unpleasant exercise, but full of delight and satisfaction. In the meantime, complain not of the hardness of the duty, but of the untowardness of thy own heart." *The Whole Duty of Man* (Lond., 1741), 122.

6. F. W. H. Myers, *Poems*.

The only remedy for this sluggish mood is that we should "rekindle our love," as Polycarp wrote to the Church in Ephesus, "in the blood of God." Let us ask for a fresh gift of the Holy Spirit to quicken our sluggish hearts, a new disclosure of the charity of God. The Spirit will help our infirmities, and the very compassion of the Son of God will fall upon us, clothing us with zeal as with a garment, stirring our affections into a most vehement flame, and filling our souls with heaven.

4. PRAYER IS CONTINUOUS

"Men ought always to pray, and"—although faintness of spirit attends on prayer like a shadow—"not faint" (Luke 18:1). The soil in which the prayer of faith takes root is a life of unbroken communion with God, a life in which the windows of the soul are always open toward the City of Rest. We do not know the true potency of prayer until our hearts are so steadfastly inclined to God that our thoughts turn to Him, as by a Divine instinct, whenever they are set free from the consideration of earthly things. It has been said of Origen (in his own words) that his life was "one unceasing supplication." By this means above all others the perfect idea of the Christian life is realized. Intercourse between the believer and his Lord ought never to be interrupted.[7]

---

7. "In our mutual intercourse and conversation—amidst all the busiest scenes of our pilgrimage—we may be moving to and fro on the rapid wing of prayer, of mental prayer—that prayer that lays the whole burden of the heart on a single sigh. A sigh breathed in the Spirit, though inaudible to all around us but God, may sanctify every conversation, every event in the history of the day. We must have fellowship at all times either with the spirit of the world or with the Spirit of God.... Prayer will be fatiguing to flesh and blood if uttered aloud and sustained long. Oral prayer, and prayer mentally ordered in words though not uttered aloud, no believer can engage in without ceasing; but there is an undercurrent of prayer that may run continually under the stream of our thoughts, and never weary us. Such prayer is the silent breathing of the Spirit of God, who dwells in our hearts (*vide* Rom. 8:9 and 1 Cor. 3:16); it is the *temper* and *habit* of the spiritual mind; it is *the pulse of our life which is hid with Christ in God.*" –Hewitson's *Life*, 100-101. "My mind was greatly fixed on Divine things: almost perpetually in the contemplation of them. I spent most of my time in thinking of Divine things, year after year; often walking alone in the woods, and solitary places, for meditation, soliloquy, and prayer, and converse with God; and it was

"The vision of God," says Bishop Westcott, "makes life a continuous prayer." And in that vision, all fleeting things resolve themselves and appear in relation to things unseen. In a broad use of the term, prayer is the sum of all the service that we render to God,[8] so that all fulfillment of duty is, in one sense, the performance of Divine service, and the familiar saying, "Work is worship," is justified. "I am prayer," said a Psalmist (Ps. 109:4). "In everything, by prayer and supplication, with thanksgiving. . . ." said an Apostle (Phil. 4:6).

In the Old Testament, that life which is steeped in prayer is often described as a walk with God. Enoch walked in assurance, Abraham in perfectness, Elijah in fidelity, the sons of Levi in peace and equity. Or it is spoken of as a dwelling with God, even as Joshua departed not from the Tabernacle (Exod. 33:11); or as certain craftsmen of the olden time abode with a king for his work (1 Kings 7:13-14). Again, it is defined as the ascent of the soul into the Sacred Presence, as the planets, "with open face beholding," climb into the light of the sun's countenance, or as a flower, lit with beauty and dipped in fragrance, reaches upward toward the light. At other times, prayer is said to be the gathering up of all the faculties in an ardor of reverence, and love, and praise. As one clear strain may succeed in reducing to harmony a number of mutually discordant voices, so the reigning impulses of the spiritual nature unite the heart to fear the name of the Lord.

But the most familiar, and perhaps the most impressive, description of prayer in the Old Testament is found in those numerous passages where the life of communion with God is spoken of as a waiting upon Him. A great scholar has given a beautiful definition of waiting upon God: "To wait is

---

always my manner to sing forth my contemplations. I was almost constantly in ejaculatory prayer, wherever I was. Prayer seemed to be natural to me, as the breath by which the inward burnings of my heart had vent." –Jonathan Edwards, *Memoirs*, ch. 1. "I see that unless I keep up short prayer every day throughout the whole day, at intervals, I lose the spirit of prayer. I would never lose sight any hour of the Lamb in the midst of the throne, and if I have this sight I shall be able to pray. –Andrew A. Bonar, *Diary*, Oct. 7, 1860.

8. Is not the name of Prayer usual to signify even all the service that ever we do God?" –Hooker, *Eccles. Polity*, v. 23.

not merely to remain impassive. It is to expect—to look for with patience, and also with submission. It is to long for, but not impatiently; to look for, but not to fret at the delay; to watch for, but not restlessly; to feel that if He does not come we will acquiesce, and yet to refuse to let the mind acquiesce in the feeling that He will not come."[9]

Now, do not let any one say that such a life is visionary and unprofitable. The real world is not this covering veil of sense; reality belongs to those heavenly things of which the earthly are mere "patterns" and correspondences. Who is so practical as God? Who among men so wisely directed His efforts to the circumstances and the occasions which He was called to face, as "the Son of Man who is in heaven" (John 3:13)? Those who pray well, work well. Those who pray most, achieve the grandest results.[10] To use the striking phrase of Tauler, "In God nothing is hindered."

5. PRAY ON ALL OCCASIONS

The cultivation of the habit of prayer will secure its expression on all suitable occasions.

In times of need, in the first instance—almost everyone will pray then. Moses stood on the shores of the Red Sea, surveying the panic into which the children of Israel were cast when they realized that the chariots of Pharaoh were thundering down upon them. "Wherefore criest thou unto Me?" said the Lord (Exod. 14:15). Nehemiah stood before King Artaxerxes. The monarch noted his inward grief, and said, "Why is thy countenance sad, seeing thou art not sick? This is nothing else but sorrow of heart." That question opened the door to admit the answer to three months' praying; and the hot desire that had risen to God in those slow months gathered itself into one fervent ejaculation: "So I prayed to the God of heaven" (Neh. 1:1-2:4).

---

9. Dr. A. B. Davidson, *Waiting upon God*, 14.

10. Compare the sentence of Thomas Hooker, of Hartford: "Prayer is the principle work of a minister, and it is by this that he must carry on the rest."

Again, one whose life is spent in fellowship with God will constantly seek and find opportunities for swift and frequently recurring approaches to the throne of grace. The apostles bring every duty under the cross; at the name of Jesus their loyal souls soar heavenward in adoration and in praise. The early Christians never met without invoking a benediction; they never parted without prayer. The saints of the Middle Ages allowed each passing incident to summon them to intercession: the shadow on the dial, the church-bell, the flight of the swallow, the rising of the sun, the falling of a leaf.

The covenant which Sir Thomas Browne made with himself is well-known, but one may venture to refer to it once more: "To pray in all places where quietness inviteth; in any house, highway, or street; and to know no street in this city that may not witness that I have not forgotten God and my Saviour in it; and that no parish or town where I have been may not say the like. To take occasion of praying upon the sight of any church which I see, or pass by, as I ride about. To pray daily, and particularly for my sick patients, and for all sick people under whose care soever. And at the entrance into the house of the sick to say, 'The peace and the mercy of God be upon this house.' After a sermon to make a prayer and desire a blessing, and to pray for the minister." And much more of a like nature.

Once more, one who lives in the spirit of prayer will spend much time in retired and intimate communion with God. It is by such a deliberate engagement of prayer that the fresh springs of devotion which flow through the day are fed. For, although communion with God is the life-energy of the renewed nature, our souls "cleave to the dust," and devotion tends to grow formal—it becomes emptied of its spiritual content and exhausts itself in outward acts. The Master reminds us of this grave peril and informs us that the true defense against insincerity in our approach to God lies in the diligent exercise of private prayer (Matt. 6:6).[11]

---

11. "Whoever is diligent in public prayers, and yet negligent in private, it is much to be feared he rather seeks to approve himself to men than to God." – *The Whole Duty of Man* (Lond., 1741), 119.

In the days of the Commonwealth, one of the early Friends, "a servant of the Lord, but a stranger outwardly," came into an assembly of serious people, who had met for worship:

> And after some time he had waited on the Lord in spirit he had an opportunity to speak, all being silent; he said by way of exhortation, "Keep to the Lord's watch." These words, being spake in the power of God, had its operation upon all or most of the meeting, so that they felt some great dread and fear upon their spirits. After a little time he spake again, saying, "What I say unto you, I say unto all, Watch" (Mark 13:37). Then he was silent again a little time, but the whole meeting, being sensible that this man was in some extraordinary spirit and power, were all musing what manner of teaching this should be, being such a voice that most of the hearers never heard before, that carried such great authority with it that they were all necessitated to be subject to the power.[12]

Soldier of Christ, you are in an enemy's country; "Keep to the Lord's watch."

---

12. Harvey's *The Rise of the Quakers*, 73-74.

Remember that in the Levitical Law there is a frequent commemoration and charge given of the two daily sacrifices, the one to be offered up in the morning and the other in the evening. These offerings by incense our holy, harmless, and undefiled High Priest hath taken away, and instead of them every devout Christian is at the appointed times to offer up a spiritual sacrifice, namely, that of prayer: for "God is a Spirit, and they that worship Him must worship Him in spirit and in truth." At these prescribed times, if thou wilt have thy prayers to ascend up before God, thou must withdraw from all outward occupations, to prepare for the inward and divine.

–Henry Vaughan, Silurist

God comes to me in silent hours,
As morning dew to summer flowers.

–Mechthild von Magdeburg

It will never be altogether well with us till we convert the universe into a prayer room, and continue in the Spirit as we go from place to place. . . . The prayer-hour is left standing before God till the other hours come and stand beside it; then, if they are found to be a harmonious sisterhood, the prayer is granted.

–George Bowen

CHAPTER 2

The Equipment

"But thou, when thou prayest, enter into thine inner chamber, and having shut thy door, pray" (Matt. 6:6 RV).

"Of this manner of prayer," says Walter Hilton of Thurgarton, "speaketh our Lord in a figure, thus: 'Fire shall always burn upon the altar, which the priest shall nourish, putting wood underneath in the morning every day, that so the fire may not go out.' That is, the fire of love shall ever be lighted in the soul of a devout and clean man or woman, the which is God's altar. And the priest shall every morning lay to it sticks, and nourish the fire; that is, this man shall by holy psalms, clean thoughts, and fervent desire, nourish the fire of love in his heart, that it may not go out at any time."[1]

The equipment for the inner life of prayer is simple, if not always easily secured. It consists particularly of a quiet place, a quiet hour, and a quiet heart.

1. A QUIET PLACE

With regard to many of us, the first of these, a quiet place, is well within our reach. But there are tens of thousands of our fellow-believers who find it generally impossible to withdraw into the desired seclusion of the secret place. A house-mother in a crowded tenement, an apprentice in city lodgings, a ploughman in his living quarters, a soldier in barracks, a boy

---

1. *The Scale of Perfection*, I. i. 1.

living at school, these and many more may not be able always to command quiet and solitude. But, "your Father knoweth." And it is comforting to reflect that the very Prince of the pilgrims shared the experience of such as these. In the carpenter's cottage in Nazareth there were, it appears, no fewer than nine persons who lived under the one roof. There were the Holy Child, Mary His mother, and Joseph. There were also the Lord's "brothers"—four of them—and at least two "sisters" (Matt. 13:55-56). The cottage consisted, let us suppose, principally of a living room, the workshop, and an inner chamber—a store-closet in which the provision for the day, the kitchen utensils, the firewood, etc., were laid. That gloomy recess had a latch on the inner side, placed there, it may be, by the carpenter's Son, for that dark chamber was His oratory, not less sacred than the cloud-wrapt shrine of the Presence in the Temple.[2]

Afterward, when our Lord had entered on His public ministry, there were occasions when He found it difficult to secure the privilege of solitude. He frequently received entertainment from those who showed Him the scantiest courtesy and afforded Him no facility for retirement. When His spirit hungered for communion with His Father, He was to bend His steps toward the rough uplands (Luke 6:12, et al):

---

2. The late Dr. John Paton, of the New Hebrides, tells of such a prayer-chamber in his father's modest dwelling: "Our home consisted of a 'but' and a 'ben,' and a mid-room, or chamber, called the 'closet'.... The 'closet' was a very small apartment betwixt the other two, having room only for a bed, a little table, and a chair, and a diminutive window shedding a diminutive light on the scene. This was the sanctuary of that cottage home. There daily, and many times a day, generally after each meal, we saw our father retire, and 'shut the door'; and we children got to understand, by a sort of spiritual instinct (for the thing was too sacred to be talked about), that prayers were being poured out there for us, as of old by the High Priest within the veil of the Most Holy Place. We occasionally heard the pathetic echoes of a trembling voice, pleading as for life, and we learned to slip out and in past that door on tip-toe, not to disturb the holy colloquy. The outside world might not know, but we knew, whence came that happy light, as of a new-born smile, that always was dawning on my father's face: it was a reflection from the Divine Presence, in the consciousness of which he lived. Never, in temple or cathedral, in mountain or in glen, can I hope to feel that the Lord God is more near, more visibly walking and talking with men, than under that humble cottage roof of thatch and oaken wattles." –Dr. John G. Paton, *Autobiography*, 10-11.

Cold mountains and the midnight air
Witnessed the fervor of His prayer.

And when, a homeless man, He came up to Jerusalem to the Feasts, it was His custom to "resort" to the olive-garden of Gethsemane (Luke 22:39). Under the laden branches of some gnarled tree, which was old when Isaiah was young, our Lord must often through the soft summer night have out-watched the stars.

Any place may become an oratory, provided that one is able to find in it seclusion. Isaac went into the fields to meditate (Gen. 25:63). Jacob lingered on the eastern bank of the Brook Jabbok, after all his company had passed over; there he wrestled with the Angel, and prevailed (Gen. 32:22-32). Moses, hidden in the clefts of Horeb, beheld the vanishing glory which marked the way by which Jehovah had gone (Exod. 33:18-23). Elijah sent Ahab down to eat and drink, while he himself withdrew to the lonely crest of Carmel (1 Kings 18:41-42). Daniel spent weeks in an ecstasy of intercession on the banks of Hiddekel (Dan. 10:1-5), which once had watered Paradise (Gen. 2:10-14). And Paul, no doubt in order that he might have an opportunity for undisturbed meditation and prayer, "was minded to go afoot" from Troas to Assos (Acts 20:13).

And if no better place presents itself, the soul which turns to God may clothe itself in quietness even in the crowded concourse or in the hurrying streets. A poor woman in a great city, never able to free herself from the insistent clamor of her little ones, made for herself a sanctuary in the simplest way. "I threw my apron over my head," she said, "and there is my closet."[3]

2. A Quiet Hour

For most of us it may be harder to find a quiet hour. I do not mean an

---

3. "On his return from West Indies to the Clyde, Hewitson was privileged to lead to Christ one of the sailors. 'I am not in want of a closet to pray in,' said he one day, as the voyage drew near its termination; 'I can just cover my face with my hat, and I am as much alone with God as in a closet.' The man had sailed from Antigua as a careless sinner." –Hewitson's *Life*, 283.

"hour" of exactly sixty minutes, but a portion of time withdrawn from the engagements of the day, fenced round from the encroachments of business or pleasure, and dedicated to God. The "world's gray fathers" might linger in the fields in meditation on the covenant-name until darkness wrapt them round. But we who live with the clang of machinery and the roar of traffic always in our ears, whose crowding obligations jostle against each other as the hours fly on, are often tempted to withdraw to other uses those moments which we ought to hold sacred to communion with heaven. Dr. Dale says somewhere that if each day had forty-eight hours, and every week had fourteen days, we might conceivably get through our work, but that, as things are, it is impossible. There is at least an edge of truth in this whimsical utterance. Certainly, if we are to have a quiet hour set down in the midst of a hurry of duties, and kept sacred, we must exercise both forethought and self-denial. We must be prepared to forgo many things that are pleasant, and some things that are profitable.[4] We shall have to redeem time, it may be from recreation, or from social interaction, or from study, or from works of benevolence, if we are to find leisure daily to enter into our closet, and having shut the door, to pray to our Father who is in secret.[5]

One is tempted to linger here, and, with all humility and earnestness, to press the consideration of this point. One sometimes hears it said, "I confess that I do not spend much time in the secret chamber, but I try to cultivate the habit of continual prayer." And it is implied that this is more and better than that. The two things ought not to be set in opposition. Each is necessary to a well-ordered Christian life; and each was perfectly maintained in the practice of the Lord Jesus. He was always enfolded in the

---

4. "Let no man that can find time to bestow upon his vanities. . .say that he wants leisure for prayer." – *The Whole Duty of Man* (Lond., 1741), 120.

5. In all his journeyings, John Wesley used to carry about with him a little note-book for jottings, the first crude draft of his *Journals*. On the front page of each successive copy of this memorandum book, he always recorded a resolution to spend two hours daily in private prayer, *no evasion or provisio being admitted*. Perhaps such a rule may seem to some to be rigid even to formality. Let no one be bound by another's practice; but in every case let due provision be made for intercourse with God.

Divine love; His communion with the Father was unbroken; He was the Son of Man who is in heaven (John 3:13). But St. Luke tells us that it was His habit to withdraw Himself into the wilderness and pray (Luke 5:16). Our Authorized Version does not at all give us the force of the original in this verse. Dean Vaughan comments on it thus: "It was not one withdrawal, nor one wilderness, nor one prayer, all is plural in the original—the withdrawals were repeated, the wildernesses were more than one, the prayers were habitual." Crowds were thronging and pressing Him; great multitudes came together to hear and to be healed of their infirmities; and He had no leisure so much as to eat (Mark 3:20). But He found time to pray. And this one who sought retirement with so much solitude was the Son of God, having no sin to confess, no shortcoming to deplore, no unbelief to subdue, no languor of love to overcome. Nor are we to imagine that His prayers were merely peaceful meditations or rapturous acts of communion. They were strenuous and warlike, from that hour in the wilderness when angels came to minister to the prostrate Man of Sorrows (Matt. 4:11), on to that awful "agony" in which His sweat was, as it were, great drops of blood (Luke 22:44). His prayers were sacrifices, offered up with strong crying and tears (Heb. 5:7).

Now, if it was part of the sacred discipline of the Incarnate Son that He should observe frequent seasons of retirement, how much more is it incumbent on us, broken as we are and disabled by manifold sin, to be diligent in the exercise of private prayer!

To hurry over this duty would be to rob ourselves of the benefits which proceed from it. We know, of course, that prayer cannot be measured by divisions of time. But the advantages to be derived from secret prayer are not to be obtained unless we enter on it with deliberation. We must "shut the door," enclosing and securing a sufficient portion of time for the fitting discharge of the engagement before us.

In the morning we should look forward to the duties of the day, anticipating those situations in which temptation may lurk, and preparing ourselves to embrace such opportunities of usefulness as may be presented to us. In the evening we ought to remark upon the providences which have befallen us, consider our attainment in holiness, and endeavor to profit by the lessons which God would have us learn. And, always, we must acknowledge and forsake sin. Then there are the numberless themes of prayer which our desires for the good estate of the Church of God, for the conversion and sanctification of our friends and acquaintances, for the furtherance of missionary effort, and for the coming of the kingdom of Christ may suggest. All this cannot be pressed into a few crowded moments. We must be at leisure when we enter the secret place. At one time at least in his life, the late Mr. Hudson Taylor was so fully occupied during the hours of the day with the direction of the China Inland Mission that he found it difficult to gain the requisite freedom for private prayer. Accordingly, he made it his rule to rise each night at two o'clock, watch with God till four, then lie down to sleep until the morning.

In the Jewish Church it was customary to set apart a space of time for meditation and prayer three times daily—in the morning, at noon, and in the evening (Ps. 55:17; Dan. 6:10). But in Bible lands there is a natural pause at mid-day which we, in our cooler climate, do not generally observe. Where it is possible to hallow a few moments in the mid-stream of the day's duties, it ought surely to be done.[6] And nature itself teaches us that morning and evening are suitable occasions of approach to God. A question which has been frequently discussed, and is not without interest is: Whether we should employ the morning or the evening hour for our more deliberate and prolonged period of waiting upon God? It is probable that each person can answer this question most profitably for himself or herself. But it should always be understood that we give our best to God.

---

6. "And here I was counseled to set up one other sail, for before I prayed but twice a day. I here resolved to set some time apart at mid-day for this effort, and, obeying this, I found the effects to be wonderful." –*Memoirs of the Rev. James Fraser* (Wodrow), 208.

3. A QUIET HEART

For most of us, perhaps, it is still harder to secure the quiet heart. The contemplationists of the Middle Ages desired to present themselves before God in silence, that He might teach them what their lips should utter and their hearts expect. Stephen Gurnall acknowledges that it is far more difficult to hang up the big bell than it is to ring it when it has been hung. McCheyne used to say that very much of his prayer time was spent in preparing to pray.[7] A New England Puritan writes, "While I was at the Word, I saw I had a wild heart, which was as hard to stand and abide before the presence of God in an ordinance, as a bird before any man." And Bunyan remarks from his own deep experience, "O! the starting-holes that the heart hath in the time of prayer; none knows how many bye-ways the heart hath and back-lanes, to slip away from the presence of God."[8]

There are, in particular, three great but simple acts of faith, which will serve to stay the mind on God.

(a) Let us, in the first place, recognize our acceptance before God through the dying of the Lord Jesus. When a pilgrim, either of the Greek or of the Latin Church, arrives in Jerusalem, his first act, before ever he seeks refreshment or rest, is to visit the traditional scene of the Redeemer's passion. Our first act in prayer ought to be the yielding of our souls to the power of the blood of Christ. It was in the power of the ritual sacrifice that the high priest in Israel passed through the veil on the Day of Atonement. It is in the power of the accepted offering of the Lamb of Divine Appointment that we are

---

7. But Fraser of Brea gives a caution respecting this which is worth remembering: "Under the pretense of waiting for the Lord for strength, I have been driven to gaze, and neglect the duty itself, when there hath been an opportunity; so in preparing for prayer I have neglected prayer." *–Memoirs*, 290.

8. "It was a saying of the martyr Bradford that he would never leave a duty till he had brought his heart into the frame of the duty; he would not leave confession of sin till his heart was broken for sin; he would not leave petitioning for grace till his heart was quickened and enlivened in a hopeful expectation of more grace; he would not leave the rendering of thanks till his heart was enlarged with the sense of the mercies which lied enjoyed and quickened in the return of praise." –Bickersteth, *A Treatise on Prayer*, 93.

privileged to come into the presence of God. "Having therefore, brethren, boldness to enter into the holy place by the blood of Jesus, by the way which He dedicated for us, a new and living way, through the veil, that is to say, His flesh; and having a Great High Priest over the house of God; let us draw near with a true heart, in fullness of faith, having our hearts sprinkled from an evil conscience, and our body washed with pure water: let us hold fast the confession of our hope that it waver not; for He is faithful that promised" (Heb. 10:19-23 RV).

> Were I with the trespass laden
> Of a thousand worlds beside,
> Yet by that path I enter—
> The blood of the Lamb who died.

(b) It is important also that we confess and receive the enabling grace of the Divine Spirit, without whom nothing is holy, nothing good. For it is He who teaches us to cry, "Abba, Father" (Rom. 8:15; Gal. 4:6), who searches for us the deep things of God (1 Cor. 2:10), who discloses to us the mind and will of Christ, who helps our infirmities and intercedes on our behalf "according to God" (Rom. 8:26).[9] And we all, "with open face beholding as in a glass the glory of the Lord, are changed into the same image from glory to glory, even as by the Spirit of the Lord" (2 Cor. 3:18). When we enter the inner chamber, we should present ourselves before God in meekness and trust and open our hearts to the incoming and infilling of the Holy Ghost. So we shall receive from the praying Spirit, and commit to the praying Christ, those petitions which are of Divine birth and express themselves, through our finite hearts

---

9. "This helping of the Spirit (Rom. 8:26) is very emphatic in the original; as a man taking up a heavy piece of timber by the one end cannot alone get it up till some other man takes it up at the other end, and so helps him; so the poor soul that is pulling and tugging with his own heart finds it heavy and dull, like a log in a ditch, and he can do no good with it, till at last the Spirit of God comes at the other end, and takes the heaviest end of the burden, and so helps the soul to lift it up." –Isaac Ambrose, *Prima Media et Ultima*, 333. Père La Combe says, "I have never found anyone who prayed so well as those who had never been taught how. They who have no master in man have one in the Holy Spirit." –*Spiritual Maxims*, 43.

and sin-stained lips, in "groanings which cannot be uttered" (Rom. 8:26). Without the support of the Holy Spirit, prayer becomes a matter of incredible difficulty. "As for my heart," said one who was deeply exercised in this engagement, "when I go to pray, I find it so loath to go to God, and when it is with Him, so loath to stay with Him, that many times I am forced in my prayers, first to beg of God that He would take mine heart, and set it on Himself in Christ, and when it is there, that He would keep it there. Nay, many times I know not what to pray for, I am so blind, nor how to pray, I am so ignorant; only, blessed be grace, the Spirit helps our infirmities."

(c) Once more, as "the Spirit rides most triumphantly in His own chariot," His chosen means of enlightenment, comfort, quickening, and rebuke being the Word of God, it is well for us in the beginning of our supplications to direct our hearts toward the Holy Scriptures. It will greatly help to calm the "contrary" mind if we open the sacred volume and read it as in the presence of God, until there shall come to us out from the printed page a word from the Eternal. George Müller confessed that often he could not pray until he had steadied his mind upon a text.[10] Is it not the prerogative of God to break the silence? "When Thou saidst, Seek ye My face; my heart said unto Thee, Thy face, Lord, will I seek" (Ps. 27:8). Is it not fitting that His will should order all the acts of our prayer with Himself? Let us be silent to God, that He may fashion us.

> So shall I keep
> For ever in my heart one silent space;
> A little sacred spot of loneliness,
> Where to set up the memory of Thy Cross,
> A little quiet garden, where no man
> May pass or rest for ever, sacred still
> To visions of Thy sorrow and Thy love.

---

10. The reader will find a striking passage, hearing on this point, in the *Autobiography of George Müller* (Lond., 1905), 152-3.

Thou oughtest to go to prayer, that thou mayest deliver thyself wholly up into the hands of God, with perfect resignation, exerting an act of faith, believing that thou art in the Divine Presence, afterward settling in that holy repose, with quietness, silence, and tranquility; and endeavoring for a whole day, a whole year, and thy whole life, to continue that first act of contemplation, by faith and love.

–Molinos

Satan strikes either at the root of faith
or at the root of diligence.

–John Livingstone

The sum is: remember always the presence of God; rejoice always in the will of God; and direct all to the glory of God.

–Archbishop Leighton

CHAPTER 3

The Direction of the Mind

In Essex, in the year 1550, a number of religious persons who had received the Word of God as their only rule of faith and conduct, and who therefore differed in certain particulars from the dominant party in the Church, met to confer on the ordering of worship. The chief point in debate related to the attitude which one ought to observe in prayer—whether it were better to stand or kneel, to have the head covered or uncovered. The decision arrived at was that the material question had reference not to the bodily posture, but to the direction of the mind. It was agreed that that attitude is most seemly which most fitly expresses the desires and emotions of the soul.

Those words of our Lord which we have prefixed to this volume (Matt. 6:6) indicate not obscurely that attitude of spirit which befits our approach to God.

1. REALIZE THE PRESENCE OF GOD

In the first place, it is necessary that we should *realize the presence of God*.[1] He who fills earth and heaven "is," in a singular and impressive sense, in the secret place. As the electric fluid which is diffused in the atmosphere

---

1. Francois de Sales says, "Always enter upon prayer by putting yourself in the Divine Presence." Gaston de Renty defines this posture of the soul as "a state of the modest presence before God, in which you maintain yourself, looking to His Spirit to suggest what He pleases to you, and receiving it in simplicity and confidence, just as if He were uttering words in your hearing." Avila, a Spanish writer on religion, tells us that "we ought to address ourselves to prayer rather in order to listen than to speak."

is concentrated in the lightning flash, so the presence of God becomes vivid and powerful in the prayer-chamber. Bishop Jeremy Taylor enforces this rule with stately and affluent speech: "In the beginning of actions of religion, make an act of adoration; that is, solemnly worship God, and place thyself in God's presence, and behold Him with the eye of faith; and let thy desires actually fix on Him as the object of thy worship, and the reason of thy hope, and the fountain of thy blessing. For when thou hast placed thyself before Him, and kneelest in His presence, it is most likely all the following parts of thy devotion will be answerable to the wisdom of such an apprehension, and the glory of such a presence."

Our Father "is" in the secret place. Then we shall find Him in the inwardness of a "recollected" spirit, in the stillness of a heart united to fear His name. The dew falls most copiously when the night-winds are hushed. The great tides lift themselves "too full for sound or foam." The suppliant who prays with a true direction of spirit, "Our Father, who art in heaven" (Matt. 6:9), is oftentimes taken up into heaven before ever he is aware. "But, oh how rare it is!" cries Fénelon, "How rare it is to find a soul quiet enough to hear God speak!" So many of us have mistrained ears. We are like the Indian hunters of whom Whittier speaks, who can hear the crackle of a twig far off in the dim forest, but are deaf to the thunder of Niagara only a few rods away. Brother Lawrence, who lived to practice the presence of God, speaks thus: "As for my set hours of prayer, they are only a continuation of the same exercise. Sometimes I consider myself there as a stone before a carver, whereof he is to make a statue; presenting myself before God, I desire Him to form His perfect image in my soul, and make me entirely like Himself. At other times, when I apply myself to prayer, I feel all my spirit and all my soul lift itself up without any care or effort of mine, and it continues as it were suspended and, firmly fixed in God, as in its center and place of rest."

The realization of the Divine presence is the inflexible condition of a right engagement of spirit in the exercise of private prayer.

John Spilsbury of Bromgrove, who was confined in Worcester jail for the testimony of Christ, bore this witness: "I shall not henceforward fear a prison as formerly, because I had so much of my Heavenly Father's company as made it a palace to me." Another, in similar case, testified, "I thought of Jesus until every stone in my cell shone like a ruby." And for us, too, in our measure, the dull room in which we talk with God, as a man may speak with his friend, will burn at times like a sapphire and a sardius stone, and be to us as the cleft rock in Sinai, through which the un-created glory poured, until the prophet's steadfast gaze was dimmed, and his countenance kindled as a flame (Exod. 34:29-35).

Our realization of the presence of God may, however, be accompanied with little or no emotion. Our spirits may lie as if dead under the hand of God. Vision and rapture may alike be withdrawn. But we ought not therefore to grow sluggish in prayer. So far from interrupting the exercise at such times, we ought to redouble our energy. And it may be that the prayer which goes up through darkness to God will bring to us a blessing such as we have not received in our most favored hours. The prayer which rises from "the land of forgetfulness," "the place of darkness," "the belly of hell," may have an abundant and glorious return.

At the same time, there are seasons of special privilege when the winds of God are unbound about the throne of grace, and the breath of spring begins to stir in the King's gardens. The Scottish preachers used to talk much of gaining access. And it is related of Robert Bruce that, when two visitors presented themselves before him on a certain morning, he said to them, "You must go and leave me for some time. I thought last night when I lay down I had a good measure of the Lord's presence, and now I have wrestled this hour or two, and have not yet got access." It may be that in his solitude there was a disproportionate subjectivity, yet the eagerness of his desire was surely commendable. To what profit is it that we dwell in Jerusalem, if we do not see the King's face? And when He comes forth from His royal chambers, accompanied with blessing, are we to hold ourselves at leisure that we may yield Him worship and offer Him service? Jonathan

Edwards resolved that whenever he should find himself "in a good frame for divine contemplation," he would not allow even the recurrence of the mid-day meal to interrupt his engagement with his Lord. "I will forgo my dinner," he said, "rather than be broke off." When the fire of God gleamed upon Carmel, it was Ahab who went down to eat and drink; it was Elijah who went up to pray (1 Kings 18:41).

2. HONESTY IN PRAYER

Again, He who "is" in the secret place "seeth" in secret, and *honest dealing becomes us* when we kneel in His pure presence.

In our address to God, we like to speak of Him as we think we ought to speak, and there are times when our words far outrun our feelings. But it is best that we should be perfectly frank before Him. He will allow us to say anything we will, so long as we say it to Himself. "I will say unto God, my rock," exclaims the psalmist, "Why hast Thou forgotten me?" (Ps. 42:9). If he had said, "Lord, Thou canst not forget: Thou hast graven my name on the palms of Thy hands" (Isa. 49:14-16), he would have spoken more worthily, but less truly. On one occasion, Jeremiah failed to interpret God aright. He cried, as if in anger, "O Lord, Thou hast deceived me, and I was deceived: Thou art stronger than I, and hast prevailed" (Jer. 20:7). These are terrible words to utter before Him who is changeless truth. But the prophet spoke as he felt, and the Lord not only pardoned him, He met and blessed him there.

It is possible that some who read these words may have a complaint against God. A controversy of long standing has come between your soul and His grace. If you were to utter the word that is trembling on your lips, you would say to him, "Why hast Thou dealt thus with me?" Then dare to say, with reverence and with boldness, all that is in your heart. "Produce your cause, saith the Lord; bring forth your strong reasons, saith the King of Jacob" (Isa. 41:21). Carry your grievance into the light of His countenance; charge your complaint home. Then listen to His answer. For surely, in gentleness and truth, He will clear Himself of the charge of unkindness that you bring against Him. And in His light you shall see light (Ps. 36:9). But, remember, that this is a private matter between you and your Lord, and you must not defame Him to any one. "If I say, I will speak thus; behold, I should offend against the generation of Thy children" (Ps. 73:15). John Livingstone of Ancrum, in a day of darkness, made a most excellent resolution: "Finding myself, as I thought, surely deserted, and somewhat hardly dealt with in my particular state, I made a promise to God not to tell it to any but Himself, lest I should seem to complain or foster misbelief in myself or others."

But there is another region in which honesty in prayer must operate. There have been times, no doubt, in the life of each one of us, when the Spirit of God granted us enlargement of affection and desire. Our prayers soared through heavenly distances, and were about to fold their wings before the throne. When, suddenly, there was brought to our remembrance some duty unfulfilled, some harmful indulgence tolerated, some sin unrepented of. It was in order that we might forsake that which is evil, and follow that which is good, that the Holy Spirit granted us so abundantly His assistance in prayer.[2] He designed that, in that good hour of His visitation, we should be enabled to purify ourselves from every stain, that henceforth we might live as His "purchased possession" (Eph. 1:14). And, perhaps, in such a case, we shunned the light, and turned back from the solicitation of God. Then darkness fell upon our face; the Divine Comforter, "who helpeth our infirmities" (Rom. 8:26), being grieved (Eph. 4:30), withdrew. And to that hour, it may be, we can trace our present feebleness in the holy exercise of prayer. "If I regard iniquity in my heart, the Lord will not hear me" (Ps. 66:18). "He that turneth away his ear from hearing the law, even his prayer is an abomination" (Prov. 28:9 RV). "Your iniquities have separated

---

2. "Prayer discovers to us the true state of our soul, for, according to theologians, it is the mirror which shows us our correct portrait." –St. John Climacus, *The Ladder of Divine Ascent*, 23.38.

between you and your God, and your sins have hid His face from you, that He will not hear" (Isa. 59:2). "And when ye spread forth your hands, I will hide Mine eyes from you; yea, when ye make many prayers, I will not hear" (Isa. 1:15). In wireless telegraphy, if the receiver is not attuned to the transmitter, communication is impossible. In true prayer, God and the suppliant must be "of one accord." Cavalier, a Huguenot leader, who had lived for years in the enjoyment of unbroken communion with God, deceived by vanity, forsook the cause to which he had devoted his life. Finally, he came to England, and entered the British army. When he was presented to Queen Anne, she said, "Does God visit you now, Monsieur Cavalier?" The young Camisard bowed his head and was silent. Christmas Evans tells of an eclipse of faith which he experienced. A time of powerlessness and decay followed. But the Lord visited him in mercy. "Lazarus had been four days dead when Jesus came that way." Immediately he began to plead that the fervor and gladness of earlier years might be restored. "On the Caerphilly mountain," he related, "the spirit of prayer fell upon me as it had once in Anglesea. I wept and supplicated, and gave myself to Christ. I wept long and besought Jesus Christ, and my heart poured forth its requests before Him on the mountain." Then followed a period of marvelous blessing.

On the other hand, "If our heart condemn us not, we have boldness toward God; and whatsoever we ask, we receive of Him, because we keep His commandments, and do the things that are pleasing in His sight" (1 John 3:21-22 RV).

The devotional writers of the Middle Ages were accustomed to distinguish between "a pure intention" and "a right intention." The former, they said, was the fruit of sanctification; the latter was the condition of sanctification. The former implied a trained and disciplined will, the latter a will laid down in meek surrender at the Master's feet. Now, what God requires of those who seek His face is "a right intention"—a deliberate, a resigned, a joyful acceptance of His good and perfect will. All true prayer must fall back upon the great atonement, in which the Man of Sorrows translated into "active passion" the supplication of His agony, "O My Father, if it be possible, let this cup pass from Me; nevertheless, not as I will, but as Thou wilt" (Matt. 26:39). He has transmitted to us His own prayer: we offer it in the power of His sacrifice. "When ye pray, say, Our Father. . . . Thy will be done" (Luke 11:2).

> Lord, here I hold within my trembling hand,
> This will of mine—a thing which seemeth small;
> And only Thou, O Christ, canst understand
> How, when I yield Thee this, I yield mine all.
> It hath been wet with tears, and stained with sighs,
> Clenched in my grasp till beauty hath it none;
> Now, from Thy footstool where it prostrate lies,
> The prayer ascendeth, "Let Thy will be done."

3. FAITH

Once more, it is necessary that when we draw near to God we should come in *faith*. "Pray to thy Father" (Matt. 6:6). "When ye pray say, Our Father" (Luke 11:2). "Fear not, little flock, for it is your Father's good pleasure to give you the kingdom" (Luke 12:32). "Your Father knoweth what things ye have need of" (Matt. 6:8). "The Father Himself loveth you" (John 16:27). The whole philosophy of prayer is contained in words like these. "This word 'Father,'" writes Luther, "hath overcome God."

(a) Let it be once admitted that with God, *no miracle is impossible*. Let it be acknowledged that He is the rewarder of them that diligently seek Him (Heb. 11:6); no true prayer will remain unblessed. But faith in God is by no means a light or trivial thing. Robert Bruce of Edinburgh used sometimes to pause in his preaching and, bending over the pulpit, say with much solemnity, "I think it's a great matter to believe there is a God." Once he confessed that during three years he had never said, "My God," without being "challenged and disquieted for the same." "These words, 'My God,'" said Ebenezer Erskine, "are the marrow of the Gospel." To be able to hold the living God within our feeble grasp, and say with assurance, "God, *even our own God*, shall bless us" (Ps. 67:6), demands a faith which is not of nature's birth.

But it is comforting to remember that even a feeble faith prevails to overcome. "Is it not a wonder," says Robert Blair, "that our words in prayer, which almost die in the coming out of our lips, should climb so well as to go into heaven?" It is indeed a wonder, but all the doings of God in grace are wondrous. Like the miner, whose trained eye detects the glitter of the precious metal sown in sparse flakes through the coarse grain of the rocks, He observes the rare but costly faith which lies imbedded in our unbelief. Standing somewhere on the slopes of that goodly mountain Hermon, our Lord said to His disciples, "If ye have faith as a grain of mustard seed, ye shall say unto this mountain, remove hence to yonder place, and it shall remove: and nothing shall be impossible unto you" (Matt. 17:20). The mountain which the word of faith was to pluck up and cast into the sea was the immeasurable mass which fills the horizon to the north of Palestine, whose roots run under the whole land of Immanuel, whose dews refresh the city of God.

> Faith, mighty faith, the promise sees,
>> And looks to that alone;
> Laughs at impossibilities,
>> And cries, It shall be done.

When the pilgrims in Bunyan's *Pilgrim's Progress* came to the Delectable Mountains, the shepherds showed them a man standing on Mount Marvel who "tumbled the hills about with words." That man was the son of one Mr. Great Grace, the King's champion, and he was set there "to teach pilgrims to believe down, or to tumble out of their ways what difficulties they should meet with, by faith."

(b) *But this God who is ours is our Father.* Our Lord confers on us His own rights and privileges. He puts into our hand the master-key, which unlocks all the doors of the treasury of God. "For however many be the promises of

God, in Him is the yea: wherefore also through Him is the Amen" (2 Cor. 1:20 RV). In Him we draw nigh to God. In Him we plead with boldness our requests. Ralph Erskine tells us that, on a certain Sabbath evening, he had unusual liberty in prayer through the name of the Lord Jesus: "I was helped to pray in secret with an outpouring of the soul before the Lord, owning my claim to the promise, my claim to pardon, my claim to grace, my claim to daily bread, my claim to a comfortable life, my claim to a stingless death, my claim to a glorious resurrection, and my claim to everlasting life and happiness: to be, only, only in Christ, and in God through Him as a promising God."

When we pray to our Father, we offer our prayers in the name of Jesus with His authority. We must not think, however, that the name of Jesus may be used by us as we like. God can in no wise deal with His children as Ahasuerus dealt with Mordecai when he handed him the great seal with the words, "Write as you like, in the king's name, and seal it with the king's ring: for the writing which is written in the king's name, and sealed with the king's ring, may no man reverse" (Esther 8:8). John Bunyan shows his accustomed spiritual discernment when, in his *Holy War*, he discourses of the petitions which the men of Mansoul sent to Emmanuel, to none of which did He return any answer. After a time "they agreed together to draw up yet another petition, and to send it away to Emmanuel for relief. But Mr. Godly-Fear stood up, and answered that he knew his Lord, the Prince, never did, nor ever would, receive a petition for these matters from the hand of any unless the Lord Secretary's hand was to it. 'And this,' quoted he, 'is the reason you prevailed not all this while.' Then they said they would draw up one, and get the Lord Secretary's hand to it. But Mr. Godly-Fear answered again that he knew also that the Lord Secretary would not set His hand to any petition that He Himself had not a hand in composing and drawing up."[3]

---

3. The petitions of believers . . . are echoes, so to speak, of the Master's own words. Their prayer is only some fragment of His teaching transformed into supplication. It must then be

The prayer of faith is a middle term between the intercession of the Holy Spirit and the intercession of Christ.[4] It is the divinely appointed means by which the unutterable groanings of the Spirit, who dwells within His people as in a temple, are conveyed and committed to the exalted Mediator, who "ever liveth to make intercession" for us (Heb. 7:25). And thus in a peculiar and especial manner those who make mention of the Lord are graced to become fellow-laborers together with God.

---

heard, for it is the expression of His will." –Bishop Westcott, on John 15:7.

4. "Prayer is heard when it passes from the believer's heart to the Redeemer's heart, and is appropriated by the Redeemer, or made His own." –W. H. Hewitson, *Life*, 375.

We praise Thee. . . . We give thanks to Thee
for Thy great glory, O Lord God.

–Book of Common Prayer

Were there nothing else For which to praise the heavens but only
love, That only love were cause enough for praise.

–Alfred, Lord Tennyson

Praise Him, ever praise Him,
For remembering dust of earth.

–Morgan Rhys

CHAPTER 4

The Engagement: Worship

"When thou has shut thy door, PRAY" (Matt. 6:6). The word used here, that word which is most frequently employed in the New Testament to denote prayer, implies "a desire toward"; and while it suggests petition, it is sufficiently general to include the whole of our engagement in the secret place—Worship, Confession, Request. In this chapter, we shall speak of the first of these—Worship.

When Scipio Africanus entered Rome, after he had humbled the proud city of Carthage, he rode in procession along the Way of Triumph, swept over the slope of the Velia, passed reverently down the ancient Way of Sacrifice, then climbed the long ascent of the Capitol, scattering with both hands "the largess of the victor," while the air was torn with the applause of the crowd. Amid the rejoicing multitudes, there were probably some whose most obvious sentiment of gratitude was stirred by the liberality of the conqueror in that hour of triumph. Others exulted in the rolling away of the terror of years and thought with emotion of the fair fields of Italy, now freed from the yoke of the stranger, while others, forgetting for the moment personal benefits or national enlargement, acclaimed the personal qualities of the victor—his resourcefulness, his benevolence, his courage, his courtesy.

Similarly, the tribute of praise which the saints are instructed to render to the Lord may arise either (1) in the acknowledgment of daily mercies, or (2) in thanksgiving for the great redemption, or (3) in contemplation of the Divine perfection.

1. ACKNOWLEDGEMENT OF DAILY MERCIES

"Memory," says Aristotle, "is the scribe of the soul." Let her bring forth her tablets, and write. Fraser of Brea, at one time a prisoner for Christ's sake on the Bass Rock, resolved that he would search out and record the loving-kindnesses of God. He did so with a very happy effect upon his own spirit. He says, "The calling to mind and serious meditating on the Lord's dealings with me as to soul and body, His manifold mercies, has done me very much good, cleared my case, confirmed my soul of God's love and my interest in Him, and made me love Him. Oh, . . . what wells of water have mine eyes been opened to see, which before were hid. Scarce anything hath done me more good than this." Let us take trouble to observe and consider the Lord's dealings with us, and we shall surely receive soul-enriching views of His kindness and truth. His mercies are new every morning. He makes the outgoings of the evening to rejoice. His thoughts concerning us are for number as the sands on the shore, and they are all thoughts of peace. Those benefits which recur with so much regularity that they seem to us "common" and "ordinary," which penetrate with golden threads the homespun vesture of our daily life, ought to be most lovingly commemorated. For, often, they are unspeakably great. "I have experienced today the most exquisite pleasure that I have ever had in my life," said a young invalid; "I was able to breathe freely for about five minutes." In Dr. Judson's house in Burma, some friends were speculating on the highest form of happiness which could arise from outward circumstances, and each fortified his own opinion by the judgment of some authority. "Pooh," said Dr. Judson, who had been recalling his terrible imprisonment in Ava. "These men were not qualified to judge. What do you think of floating down the Irrawadi, on a cool, moonlight evening, with your wife by your side, and your baby in your arms, free, all free? But you cannot understand it either; it needs a twenty-one months' qualification; and I can scarcely regret my twenty-one months of misery when I recall that one delicious thrill. I think I have had a better appreciation of what heaven may be ever since." But how often do we thank God for the mere joy of living in the free and healthful use of all our faculties?

"The river past, and God forgotten," is an English proverb which ought in no case to apply to those who have tasted that the Lord is gracious. "Praise is comely for the upright" is the judgment of the Old Testament (Ps. 33:1); "In everything give thanks" is the decision of the New (1 Thess. 5:18). Even a heathen was moved to say, "What can I, a lame old man, do but sing His praise, and exhort others to do the same?"[1] For the beauty of nature, the fellowship of the good, the tender love of home; for safe conduct in temptation, strength to overcome, deliverance from evil; for the generosity, the patience, the sympathy of God; and for ten thousand thousand unobserved or unremembered mercies, let us unweariedly bless His Holy Name. "Oh, give thanks unto the Lord; for He is good; for His mercy endureth for ever" (Ps. 136:1).[2]

But if things go hard with us, and trials darken all our sky, are we still to give thanks, and bless our God? Most surely.

> Trials make the promise sweet;
>> Trials give new life to prayer;
> Trials bring me to His feet,
>> Lay me low, and keep me there.

Let us thank God for our trials. We dwell, perhaps, in a land of narrowness. But, like Immanuel Kant's garden, it is "endlessly high." The air is fresh, and the sun is clear. The winter is frosty, but kindly. With the springtime come the singing of birds and the bloom and fragrance of flowers. And if, even in the summer, there breathes "a nipping and an eager air," there is always the health-giving smile of God. On the other hand, how true is the sentence of

---

1. Epictetus, *Eph.* 1:6

2. Richard Baxter advises that on Sabbath days we should be briefer in confession and lamentation and give ourselves more to prayer and thanksgiving (*Method of Peace and Comfort*). It was Grimshaw's custom to begin his morning devotions by singing the doxology. Of Joseph Alleine it was said, "Such was the vehement heaviness of his spirit, that his favorite employment was praise."

Augustine, "Earthly riches are full of poverty." Rich stores of corn and wine will never satisfy a hungry soul. Purple and fine linen may only mask a threadbare life. The shrill blare of fame's trumpet cannot subdue the discords of the spirit. The best night that Jacob ever spent was that in which a stone was his pillow and the skies the curtains of his tent (Gen. 28:10-22). When Job was held in derision by youths whose fathers he would have disdained to set with the dogs of his flock (Job 30:1), he was made a spectacle to angels and became the theme of their wonder and joy. The defeat which Adam sustained in Paradise, the Redeemer retrieved in the desolation of the desert and the anguish of His passion. The cross we are called to bear may be heavy, but we have not to carry it far. And when God bids us lay it down, heaven begins.

Chrysostom, on his way to exile, exclaimed, "Thank God for everything." If we imitate him we shall never have a bad day. Alexander Simson, a famous Scottish minister of two hundred years ago, once when out walking fell and broke his leg. He was found "sitting with his broken leg in his arm, and always crying out, 'Blessed be the Lord; blessed be His name.' " And truly, seeing that all things work together for good to those who love God (Rom. 8:28), he was wise. Richard Baxter found reason to bless God for a discipline of pain which endured for five-and-thirty years. And Samuel Rutherford exclaims, "Oh, what owe I to the furnace, the file, and the hammer of my Lord Jesus!"

2. Thanksgiving for Redemption

But all our mercies, rightly viewed, lead us back to the thought of our acceptance in Christ. The river of the water of life, which makes the desert glad, flows from under the throne of God and the Lamb (Rev. 22:1). The benefits of that gracious covenant that is ordered and sure are all confirmed for our use and pleasure by the blood-seal.

> There's not a gift His hand bestows,
>   But cost His heart a groan.

The water may be spent in the bottle, but the Well of the Oath is springing freshly just at hand, so near that we may hear the music of its flow. Thieves may rob us of our spending money, "but our gold is in our trunk at home." God may take away from us much that is dear, but has He not given us Christ? And however the prayer of thanksgiving may circle in and out among the gracious providences of God, it will infallibly come to rest at the feet of the Lord.

But to praise Christ is a high exercise. What Thomas Boston says of preaching is as true of praising: "I saw the preaching of Christ to be the most difficult thing; for that, though the whole world is full of wonders, yet here are depths beyond all." And seeing it to be so, he kept this "suit" depending before God for a long time, "That he might see Christ by a spiritual illumination." So eager was he for the acceptance of his plea, and so grievous to his soul was his ignorance of Christ, that his bodily health began to be affected. Yet, as he tells us, there were times when his soul went out in love to Christ, followed hard after Him, and "saw much content, delight, and sweet in Him."

The Passover in Israel was celebrated on the eve of the great deliverance, which was thenceforth a "night to be much observed unto the Lord" (Exod. 12:42). Let us frequently commemorate our redemption from a bondage more bitter than that of Egypt. John Bunyan conveys this wholesome counsel to his "dear children": "Call to mind the former days and years of ancient times; remember also your songs in the night, and commune with your own hearts. Yea, look diligently, and leave no corner therein unsearched, for that treasure hid, even the treasure of your first and second experience of the grace of God toward you; remember, I say, the word that first laid hold upon you; remember your terrors of conscience and fear of death and hell; remember also your tears and prayers to God—yea, how you sighed under every hedge for mercy! Have you never a hill Mizar to remember? Have you forgot the closet, the milk-house, the stable, the barn, and the like, where God did visit your souls? Remember also the word—the word, I say, upon which the Lord caused you to hope."

It is right also that we should search into the riches and glory of the inheritance of which we have been made partakers. The blood of Christ, the grace of the Spirit, the light of the Divine countenance, are "three jewels worth more than heaven. The name of Christ hath in it ten thousand treasures of joy."[3] Perhaps the most acceptable form of worship and the swiftest incitement to praise, when we recall the mercies which are made sure to us "in the blood of an eternal covenant" (Heb. 13:20), is the act of appropriation by which we serve ourselves heirs to the purchased possession already ours in Christ. Dr. Chalmers was one of those who discovered this open secret. In his diary we frequently meet with expressions such as these: "Began my first waking minutes with a confident hold of Christ as my Saviour. A day of great quietness." "Let the laying hold of Christ as my propitiation be the unvarying initial act of every morning." "Began the day with a distinct act of confidence; but should renew it through the day." "Began again with an act of confidence; but why not a perennial confidence in the Saviour?" "I have recurred more frequently to the actings of faith in Christ, and I can have no doubt of this being the habit that is to bring me right." "Recurring to the topic of a large confidence and belief in the promises of the Gospel, let me act on the injunction, 'Open thy mouth wide, and I will fill it.'"

It is our pleasant duty also to review with thanksgiving all the way by which the Lord has led us. Otto Funcke has beautifully entitled his brief autobiography *The Footprints of God in the Pathway of My Life*. The way of the Divine direction may lead from the bitter waters of Marah to the tempered shade of Elim's palms. It may pass through the fiery desert, but it reaches onwards to the Mount of God. It may descend to the valley of the shadow of death, but it will bring us out and through to the pleasant land of the promises of God—

A land of corn and wine and oil,
Favored with God's peculiar smile,
With every blessing blest.

3. Chrysostom, quoted by Thomas Watson

And in that "right way" of the Divine conduct, there is always the comforting and adorable presence of our Great God and Saviour. We cannot recall the mercies of the way and not remember Him. He took, with a hand that was pierced, the bitter cup, and drank, until His lips were wet with our sorrow and doom. And now the cup of bitterness has become sweet. Where His footsteps fell the wilderness rejoiced, and the waste places of our life became fruitful as Carmel. A rugged track beneath our feet ran darkly into the night, but the tender love of His presence was as a lamp to our feet and a light upon our path. His name is fragrance, His voice is music, His countenance is health. Dr. Judson, in his last illness, had a wonderful entrance into the land of praise. He would suddenly exclaim, as the tears ran down his face, "Oh, the love of Christ! The love of Christ! We cannot understand it now, but what a beautiful study for eternity." Again and again, though his pain was constant and severe, he would cry in a holy rapture, "Oh, the love of Christ! The love of Christ!"

Such praises uplift their strain until it mingles with the glory of the new song which fills the sanctuary on high, "Thou art worthy to take the book, and to open the seals thereof: for Thou wast slain, and hast redeemed us to God by Thy blood, out of every kindred, and tongue, and people, and nation; and hast made us unto our God kings and priests: and we shall reign on the earth" (Rev. 5:9-10).

3. CONTEMPLATION OF THE DIVINE PERFECTION

And so, praise addressed to God in name and memory of Jesus Christ rises inevitably into adoration. And here, most often, "praise is silent." Isaiah, transported by faith into the inner sanctuary, was rapt into the worship of the seraphim and joined in spirit in the unending adoration of the Triune God—"Holy, holy, holy, is the Lord of hosts: the whole earth is full of His glory" (Isa. 6:3). The herald angels poured forth upon the plains of Bethlehem the song of heaven, "Glory to God in the highest" (Luke 2:14); and our sad earth heard and was comforted.

Angels, help us to adore Him;
Ye behold Him face to face!

But even these bright intelligences are unable to show forth all His praise.[4]

It is reported of John Janeway that often in the hour of secret prayer he scarcely knew whether he were "in the body, or out of the body." Tersteegen said to some friends who had gathered round him, "I sit here and talk with you, but within is the eternal adoration, unceasing and undisturbed." Woodrow relates that on one occasion Mr. Carstairs was invited to take part in communion services at Calder, near Glasgow. He was wonderfully assisted, and had "a strange gale through all the sermon." His hearers were affected in an unusual degree; glory seemed to fill the house. "A Christian man that had been at the table, and was obliged to come out of the church, pressing to get in again, could not succeed for some time, but stood without the door, wrapt up in the thoughts of that glory that was in the house, for nearly half-an-hour, and could think of nothing else."

Dr. A. J. Gordon describes the impression made upon his mind by dialogue with Joseph Rabinowitz, whom Dr. Delitzsch considered the most remarkable Jewish convert since Saul of Tarsus: "We shall not soon forget the radiance that would come into his face as he expounded the Messianic psalms at our morning or evening worship, and how, as here and there he caught a glimpse of the suffering or glorified Christ, he would suddenly lift his hands and his eyes to heaven in a burst of admiration, exclaiming with Thomas, after he had seen the nail-prints, 'My Lord, and my God!' "

With many of us, emotion may be feeble, and rapture of the spirit may be rare. Love to Christ may express itself more naturally in right conduct than in a tumult of praise. But it is probable that to each sincere believer there are granted seasons of communion when, as one turns to the unseen glory, the veil of sense becomes translucent, and one seems to behold within the

---

4. No doubt the angels think themselves as insufficient for the praises of the Lord as we do." –*John Livingston's Diary*, 14 Dec. 1634 (Wodrow Society)

Holiest the very Face and Form of Him who died for our sins, who rose for our justification, who now awaits us at the right hand of God. But, even so, we must never forget that adoration does not exhaust itself in pleasing emotions. By the law of its nature it turns again to request: "Our Father, which art in heaven, hallowed be Thy name" (Matt. 6:9).

The garden of spices is sprinkled with red flowers.

–Heinrich Seuse

It is a great and rare thing to have forgiveness in God discovered unto a sinful soul. . . . It is a pure Gospel truth, that hath neither shadow, footstep, nor intimation elsewhere. The whole creation hath not the least obscure impression of it left thereon.

–John Owen

Before His breath the bands
    That held me fall and shrivel up in flame.
He bears my name upon His wounded hands,
    Upon His heart my name.

"I wait, my soul doth wait
    For Him who on His shoulder bears the key;
I sit fast bound, and yet not desolate;
    My mighty Lord is free.

"Be thou up-lifted, Door
    Of everlasting strength! the Lord on high
Hath gone, and captive led for evermore
    My long captivity.

–Dora Greenwell

CHAPTER 5

The Engagement: Confession

"If we confess our sins, He is faithful and just to forgive us our sins, and to cleanse us from all unrighteousness" (1 John 1:9). Confession of sin is the first act of an awakened sinner, the first mark of a gracious spirit. When God desires an habitation in which to dwell, He prepares "a broken and a contrite heart" (Isa. 66:2). The altar of reconciliation stands at the entrance of the New Testament temple; from the altar the worshipper passes on, by way of the laver, to the appointed place of meeting: the blood-stained mercy-seat.

But we speak now rather of the confession of sin which is due by those who are justified, having found acceptance in Christ Jesus. Though they are children, they are sinners still. And if they walk in the light, they are conscious—as in their unregenerate state they never were—of the baseness of their guilt, the hatefulness of their iniquity. For now they bring their transgressions and apostasies into the light of God's countenance, and holding them up before Him, cry, "Against Thee, Thee only, have I sinned, and done this evil in Thy sight: that Thou mightest be justified when Thou speakest, and be clear when Thou judgest" (Ps. 51:4).

1. BE EXPLICIT

Confession of sin should be explicit. "The care of Christianity is for particulars," says Bishop Warburton. The ritual law in Israel which provided for the transference of sin on the Day of Atonement pre-supposed definiteness of confession: "Aaron shall lay both his hands upon the head of the live goat, and confess over him all the iniquities of the children of Israel, and all their transgressions in all their sins" (Lev. 16:21). In private sacrifices, also, while the hands of the offerer were laid on the victim (Lev. 1:4), the following prayer was recited: "I entreat, O Jehovah: I have sinned, I have done perversely, I have rebelled, I have committed _____"; then the special sin, or sins, were named, and the worshipper continued, "but I return in penitence: let this be for my atonement." Standing beside the ruins of Jericho, Joshua said to Achan, "My son, give, I pray thee, glory to the Lord God of Israel, and make confession unto Him." And Achan answered, "Indeed, I have sinned against the Lord God of Israel; and thus and thus have I done" (Josh. 7:19-20). The great promise of the New Testament is not less definite: "If we confess our sins, He is faithful and just to forgive us our sins, and to cleanse us from all unrighteousness" (1 John 1:9). A wise old writer says, "A child of God will confess sin in particular; an unsound Christian will confess sin by wholesale; he will acknowledge he is a sinner in general; whereas David doth, as it were, point with his finger to the sore: 'I have done this evil' (Ps. 51:4); he doth not say, 'I have done evil,' but 'this evil.' He points to his blood-guiltiness."

When, in the course of the day's engagements, our conscience witnesses against us that we have sinned, we should at once confess our guilt, claim by faith the cleansing of the blood of Christ, and so wash our hands in innocence. And afterward, as soon as we have a convenient opportunity, we ought to review with deliberation the wrong that we have done. As we consider it with God, we shall be impressed by its sinfulness, as we were not at the time of its committal. And if the sin is one which we have committed before, one to which perhaps our nature lies open, we must cast ourselves in utter faith upon the strong mercy of God, pleading with Him in the name of Christ that we may never again so grieve Him.[1]

---

1. "Think of the *guilt of sin*, that you may be humbled. Think of the *power of sin*, that you may seek strength against it. Think not of the *matter of sin* . . . lest you be more and more entangled." –John Owen

As our hearts grow more tender in the presence of God, the remembrance of former sins which have already been acknowledged and forgiven will from time to time imprint a fresh stain upon our conscience. In such a case nature itself seems to teach us that we ought anew to implore the pardoning grace of God. For we bend, not before the judgment seat of the Divine Lawgiver, but before our Father, to whom we have been reconciled through Christ. A more adequate conception of the offense which we have committed ought surely to be followed by a deeper penitence for the wrong done. Under the guidance of the Holy Spirit we shall often be led to pray with the Psalmist, "Remember not the sins of my youth" (Ps. 25:7), even though these have long since been dealt with and done away. Conviction of sin will naturally prompt to confession. When such promptings are disregarded, the Spirit who has wrought in us that conviction is grieved.

> My sins, my sins, my Saviour,
>> How sad on Thee they fall;
> While through Thy gentle patience
>> I ten-fold feel them all.
> I know they are forgiven;
>> But still their pain to me
> Is all the grief and anguish
> They laid, my Lord, on Thee.

2. YIELD TO THE COMFORTER

It is of the first importance that in all the exercises of the secret chamber we should yield ourselves to the blessed influences of the Comforter, by whom alone we are enabled to pray with acceptance. An important caution in regard to this has been noted by Ralph Erskine. In his diary, he writes, under the date January 23, 1733: "This morning I was quickened in prayer, and strengthened to hope in the Lord. At the beginning of my prayer I discerned a lively frame in asserting a God in Christ to be the fountain of my life, the strength of my life, the joy of my life; and that I had no life that deserved that name, unless He Himself were my life. But here, checking myself with reflections upon my own sinfulness, vileness, and corruption, I began to acknowledge my wickedness; but for the time the sweetness of frame failed me, and wore off. Whence, I think, I may gather this lesson, that no sweet influence of the Spirit ought to be checked upon pretense of getting a frame better founded upon humiliation; otherwise, the Lord may be provoked to withdraw." When Thomas Boston found himself in danger of giving way to vain-glory, he took a look at his black feet.[2] We may well do the same, but never so as to lose our assurance of sonship or our sense of the preciousness of Christ. As Rutherford reminds us, "There is no law-music in heaven: there all their song is, "Worthy is the Lamb." And the blood of ransom has atoned for ALL SIN.

Believers of a former age used to observe with thankfulness the occasions on which they were enabled to show "a kindly, penitential mourning for sin." At other times, they would lament their deadness. Yet it never occurred to them that the coldness of their affections should induce them to restrain prayer before God. On the contrary, they were of one mind with "a laborious and successful wrestler at the throne of grace," who determined that "he would never give over enumerating and confessing his sins, till his heart were melted in contrition and penitential sorrow."

3. Why Deadness of Heart?

For such deadness of heart there may be many explanations.

He who was once as a flame of fire in his Master's service may have allowed the fervor of his first love to decline for want of fuel, or want of watchful care, until only a little heap of gray ashes smolders on the altar of his affections. His greatest sorrow is that he has no sorrow for sin, his

---

2. The biographer of Charles Simeon, of Cambridge, remarks, "Simeon in his private hours was peculiarly broken and prostrate before the Lord."

heaviest burden that he is unburdened. "Oh, that I were once again under the terrors of Christ," was the cry of one who had hung in agony over the brink of the pit, but who had learned that a cold heart towards Christ is still more insupportable. Those who are in such a case are often nearer the Saviour than they know. Shepard of New England, speaking from a wide experience, says, "More are drawn to Christ under the sense of a dead, blind heart, than by all sorrows, humiliations, and terrors."

That which impresses us as deadness of heart may be the operation of the Holy Spirit, convincing us of sins hitherto unnoticed. As one looks at some star-galaxy, and sees it only as a wreath of dimming mist, so one becomes conscious of innumerable unregarded sins, merely by the shadow which they fling upon the face of the heavens. But when one observes through a telescope the nebulous drift, it resolves itself into a cluster of stars, almost infinite in number. And when one examines in the secret place of communion the cloud which darkens the face of God, it is seen to scatter and break into a multitude of sins. If, then, in the hour of prayer we have no living communion with God, let us plead with the psalmist, "Search me, O God, and know my heart; try me, and know my thoughts; and see if there be any way of wickedness in me, and lead me in the way everlasting" (Ps. 139:23-24 RV). He who has engaged to "search Jerusalem with candles" (Zeph. 1:12) will examine us through and through, will test us as silver is proved, will sift us as wheat. He will bring up from the unexplored depths of our nature all that is contrary to the mind of Christ and reduce every thought and imagination to the obedience of His will.

Deadness of heart may arise also from the consciousness of our many sins of omission—duties unattempted, opportunities unimproved, grace disregarded. Often, when we kneel in prayer, "the lost years cry out" behind us. What was related of Archbishop Ussher might be said of very many of the Lord's servants—"He prayed often, and with great humility, that God would forgive him his sins of omission, and his failings in his duty." Each day is a vessel to be freighted with holy deeds and earnest endeavors before it weighs anchor and sets sail for the eternal shores. How many hours we misspend! How many occasions we lose! How many precious gifts of God we squander! And the world passes away, and the fashion of it fadeth.

But there is that which lies still deeper in the soul than even secret sin—there is native sinfulness, the body of death. When we acknowledge the depravity of our nature, we should endeavor to speak according to the measure of our experience. We can scarcely exaggerate the facts, but we may easily overstate our appreciation of them. As we advance in grace, as we become accustomed to hold our lightest thought or feeling within the piercing illumination of the Divine purity, as we open the most hidden recesses of our being to the gracious influences of the good Spirit of God, we are led into a profounder understanding of the sinfulness of inbred sin, until we lament with Ezra, "Oh, my God, I am ashamed, and blush to lift up my face to Thee, my God" (Ezra 9:6).

It is reported of Luther that for one long day his inborn sinfulness revealed itself in dreadful manifestations, so vehement and terrifying that "the very venom of them drank up his spirits, and his body seemed dead, that neither speech, sense, blood, or heat appeared in him." On a day of special fasting and prayer, Thomas Shepard of Cambridge, Connecticut, wrote as follows: "November 3rd. I saw sin as my greatest evil; and that I was vile; but God was good only, whom my sins did cross. And I saw what cause I had to loathe myself.... The Lord also gave me some glimpse of myself; a good day and time it was to me.... I went to God, and rested on Him.... I began to consider whether all the country did not fare the worse for my sins. And I saw it was so. And this was an humbling thought to me." President Edwards had at one time an amazing discovery of the beauty and glory of Christ. After recording it in his diary, he continues: "My wickedness, as I am in myself, has long appeared to me perfectly ineffable, and swallowing up all thought and imagination, like an infinite deluge, or mountains over my head. I know not how to express better what my sins appear to me to be, than by heaping infinite upon infinite, and multiplying infinite by infinite.

Very often for these many years these expressions are in my mind and in my mouth, 'Infinite upon infinite! Infinite upon infinite!'" When Dr. John Duncan was drawing near to death, he remarked with great earnestness, "I am thinking with horror of the carnal mind, enmity against God. I never get a sight of it but it produces horror, even bodily sickness."

These are solemn experiences. Perhaps God leads few of His children through waters so wild and deep. Nor must we try to follow, unless He points the way. Above all, we dare not, in confessions which are addressed to a holy God, simulate an experience which we have never known. But let us, as far as God has revealed it to us, confess the deep sin of our nature. It has been said with much truth that the only "sign of one's being in Christ which Satan cannot counterfeit" is the grief and sorrow which true believers undergo when God discloses to them the sinfulness of inbred sin.[3]

But, on the other hand, the love of Christ at times so fills the heart that, though the remembrance of sin continues, the sense of sin is lost— swallowed up in a measureless ocean of peace and grace. Such high moments of visitation from the living God are surely a prelude to the joy of heaven. For the song of the redeemed in glory is unlike the praises of earth in this, that while it also celebrates the death of the Lamb of God there is in it no mention of sin. All the poisonous fruits of our iniquity have been killed; all the bitter consequences of our evil deeds have been blotted out. And the only relics of sin which are found in heaven are the scarred feet and hands and side of the Redeemer. So, when the saved from earth recall their former transgressions, they look to Christ; and the remembrance of sin dies in the love of Him who wore the thorny-crown and endured the cross.

> The fouler was the error,
> > The sadder was the fall,
> The ampler are the praises
> > Of Him who pardoned all.

---

3. Dr. Payson, *Lift*, 79.

Make me sensible of real answers to actual requests, as evidence of an interchange between myself on earth and my Saviour in heaven.

–Thomas Chalmers

O brother, pray; in spite of Satan, pray; spend hours in prayer; rather neglect friends than not pray; rather fast, and lose breakfast, dinner, tea, and supper—and sleep too—than not pray. And we must not talk about prayer, we must pray in right earnest. The Lord is near. He comes softly while the virgins slumber.

–A. A. Bonar

The main lesson about prayer is just this: Do it! Do it! Do it! You want to be taught to pray. My answer is: pray and never faint, and then you shall never fail. There is no possibility. You cannot fail. . . . A sense of real want is the very root of prayer.

–John Laidlaw

CHAPTER 6

The Engagement: Request

Once, when the late Dr. Moody Stuart happened to be in Huntly, Duncan Matheson took him to see some earnest Christian people. He visited, among others, an aged woman who was in her own way a "character." Before leaving, he prayed with her; and she, as her habit was, emphasized each petition with some ejaculatory comment or note of assent. Toward the close of his prayer, he asked that God, according to His promise, would give her "all things." The old lady interjected, "All things, na, that wad be a lift." The mingling of comfort and doubt which was revealed by the quaint insertion is characteristic of the faith of very many of the children of God when they are brought face to face with some great promise addressed to believing prayer: "And all things whatsoever ye shall ask in prayer, believing, ye shall receive" (Matt. 21:22); "Therefore I say unto you, All things whatsoever ye pray and ask for, believe that ye have received them, and ye shall have them" (Mark 11:24 RV); "If ye abide in Me, and My words abide in you, ask whatsoever ye will, and it shall be done unto you" (John 15:7 RV). It is so reasonable to think that He who spared not His own Son should with Him also freely give us all things (Rom. 8:32); and it is so hard to believe that He will. As Dr. Moody Stuart says elsewhere, the controversy is between the mustard-seed and the mountain: "The trial is whether the mountain shall bury the mustard-seed, or the mustard-seed cast the mountain into the sea." The mustard-seed is so small, and the mountain so great, that faith is not easily come by. Indeed, it is literally "the gift of God" (Eph. 2:8). It is a divinely-implanted persuasion, the fruit of much spiritual instruction and discipline. It is vision in a clearer light than that of earth.

1. A DISPOSITION CONFORMED TO THE MIND OF CHRIST

The prayer of faith, like some plant rooted in a fruitful soil, draws its virtue from a disposition which has been brought into conformity with the mind of Christ.

(a) It is subject to the Divine will—"This is the confidence that we have in Him, that, if we ask anything according to His will, He heareth us" (1 John 5:14).

(b) It is restrained within the interest of Christ—"Whatsoever ye shall ask in My name, that will I do, that the Father may be glorified in the Son" (John 14:13).

(c) It is instructed in the truth—"If ye abide in Me, and My words abide in you, ye shall ask what ye will, and it shall be done unto you" (John 15:7).

(d) It is energized by the Spirit—"Able to do exceeding abundantly above all that we ask or think, according to the power that worketh in us" (Eph. 3:20).

(e) It is interwoven with love and mercy—"And when ye stand praying, forgive, if ye have ought against any; that your Father also which is in heaven may forgive you your trespasses" (Mark 11:25).

(f) It is accompanied with obedience—"Whatsoever we ask, we receive of Him, because we keep His commandments, and do those things that are pleasing in His sight" (1 John 3:22).

(g) It is so earnest that it will not accept denial—"Ask, and it shall be given you; seek, and ye shall find; knock, and it shall be opened unto you" (Luke 11:9; cf. vs. 5-8).

(h) It goes out to look for and hasten its answer—"The supplication of a righteous man availeth much in its working" (James 5:16 RV).[1]

---

1. "In prayer we tempt God if we ask for that which we labor not for; our faithful endeavors must second our devotion.... If we pray for grace and neglect the spring from whence it comes, how can we speed? It was a rule in ancient times, 'Lay thy hand to the plow, and then pray.' No man should pray without plowing, nor plow without prayer." R. Sibbes, *Divine Meditations*, 174.

2. The Warrant for Faith

But, although the prayer of faith springs from a divinely-implanted disposition, there is nothing mysterious in the act of faith. It is simply an assurance which relies upon a sufficient warrant.

(a) In the first instance, the warrant of faith is *the Word of God*. The promises of God are letters of credit, drawn on the bank of heaven, to be honoured at sight. Some time ago, a bundle of Bank of England notes was stolen, but they were unsigned, and therefore valueless. But the promises of God are all witnessed to by the eternal veracity and are countersigned in the blood of the cross. They are subject to no discount; those who present them will receive their full face-value. "I am the Lord; I will speak, and the word that I shall speak shall be performed."

(b) The Word of God rests on *the Divine character*. Therefore we are taught to pray, "O Lord, do Thou it, for Thy name's sake." God is our Father, and He knoweth what things we have need of (Matt. 6:8). He is our God in covenant—our own God—and He will bless us. He is the God and Father of our Lord Jesus Christ, and He will secure to His well-beloved Son the inheritance which He has purchased in blood. He is the source of blessing, from whom the Comforter proceeds, and the prayer which He inspires He will fulfill.

In the intercession of Daniel the prophet, we have a signal illustration of petitions founded on this two-fold warrant. He "understood by books the number of the years, whereof the word of the Lord came to Jeremiah the prophet, that He would accomplish seventy years in the desolations of Jerusalem" (Dan. 9:2). But the prophet does not rest His trust only on the promise; he urges that which is due to the Divine character: "Now, therefore, O our God, hearken unto the prayer of Thy servant, and to his supplications, and cause Thy face to shine upon Thy sanctuary that is desolate, for the Lord's sake. O my God, incline Thine ear, and hear; open Thine eyes, and behold our desolations, and the city which is called by Thy name: for we do not present our supplications before Thee for our righteousness, but for Thy great mercies. O Lord, hear; O Lord, forgive; O Lord, hearken and do; defer not; for Thine own sake, O my God, because Thy city and Thy people are called by Thy name" (Dan. 9:17-19).

3. REASONS WHY WE MUST PRAY

But it may be objected, "If our Father knoweth what things we have need of before we ask Him (Matt. 6:8), and if it is His good pleasure to give us the kingdom (Luke 12:32), is it necessary that we should present our petitions deliberately before Him?" The simplest answer to that question is that *we are instructed to do so.* In the Old Testament we read, "Thus saith the Lord God, I will yet for this be inquired of by the house of Israel, to do it for them" (Ezek. 36:37). And in the New Testament, "In everything by prayer and supplication, with thanksgiving, let your requests be made known unto God" (Phil. 4:6). We have a striking illumination of the working of this Divine law in the case of Elijah (1 Kings 18). He had preserved unhesitating fidelity toward God, and so had fulfilled the conditions by which alone fellowship with the Holy One is secured and maintained—"Jehovah liveth, before whom I stand" (v. 15). He had won Israel back to covenant allegiance—"And when all the people saw it, they fell on their faces; and they said, The Lord, He is the God; the Lord, He is the God" (v. 39). He had received and acted upon a definite promise—"Go, show thyself unto Ahab; and I will send rain upon the earth" (v. 1). He had the inward assurance that God's answer to his long-continued importunity of prayer was already on its way—"There is a sound of abundance of rain" (v. 41). Nevertheless, he did not cease from praying—he could not until the skies grew dark with the gathering storm (vs. 42-46).

It is possible, however, to suggest certain reasons why we should, with particularity and importunity, implore those blessings which are already ours in Christ.

(a) By prayer *our continued and humble dependence* on the grace of God is secured. If the bestowments of the covenant came to us without solicitation, as the gifts of nature do, we might be tempted to hold ourselves in independence of God, to say, "My power, and the might of mine hand, hath gotten me this wealth" (Deut. 8:17).[2]

(b) The Lord desires to have us much in *communion with Himself.*[3] The reluctance of the carnal heart to dwell in God's presence is terrible. We will rather speak of Him than to Him. How often He finds occasion to reprove us, saying, "The companions hearken to thy voice; cause Me to hear it" (Song 8:13). A father will prize an ill-spelled, blotted scrawl from his little child, because it is a pledge and seal of love.[4] And precious in the sight of the Lord are the prayers of His saints.

(c) Much, very much, has often to be accomplished in us before we are fitted to employ worthily the gifts we covet. And God effects this preparation of heart largely by delaying to grant our request at once, and so holding us in the truth of His presence until we are brought into a *spiritual understanding of the will of Christ* for us in this respect. If a friend, out of his way (Luke 11:6, marg.), comes to us, hungry and seeking from us the bread of life, and we have nothing to set before him, we must go to Him who has all store of blessing. And if He should seem to deny our prayer, and say, "Trouble Me not," it is only that we may understand the nature of the blessing we seek and be fitted to dispense aright the bounty of God.

(d) Once more, we are called to be *fellow-laborers together with God,*

---

2. "Prayer not only obtains mercies; it sweetens and sanctifies them." –Flavel, *Works*, 5:351 "God does not delay to hear our prayers, because He has no mind to give; but that, by enlarging our desires, He may give us the more largely." –Anselm of Canterbury

3. "We must draw off from prayer, from resting in it, or trusting upon it; a man may pray much, and instead of drawing nigh to God, or enjoying sweet communion with Christ, he may draw nigh to prayer, his thoughts may be more upon his prayer than upon God to whom he prays; and he may live more upon his cushion than upon Christ; but when a man indeed draws nigh to God in prayer, he forgets prayer, and remembers God, and prayer goes for nothing, but Christ is all." –Isaac Ambrose, *Prima Media et Ultima*, 332.

4. "The brief, childlike letters that were sent to him by them [his sons] were bound up into a paper volume, which he carried about with him during his Mongolian wanderings, and in looking over them he found an unfailing solace and refreshment." –*Life of Gilmour of Mongolia*, 241, 251.

in prayer, as in all other ministries. The exalted Saviour ever lives to make intercession; and to His redeemed people He says, "Tarry ye here, and watch with Me" (Matt. 26:38). There is a great work to be done in the hearts of men; there is a fierce battle to be waged with spiritual wickedness in heavenly places. Demons are to be cast out, the power of hell to be restrained, the works of the devil to be destroyed. And in these things, it is by prayer above all other means that we shall be able to co-operate with the Captain of the Lord's host.[5]

> God spake, and gave us the word to keep;
> Bade never fold the hands, nor sleep
> 'Mid a faithless world—at watch and ward,
> Till Christ at the end relieve our guard.
> By His servant Moses the watch was set;
> Though near upon cock-crow we keep it yet.

(e) When prayer rises to its true level, *self, with its concerns and needs, is for the time forgotten*, and the interests of Christ fill, and sometimes overwhelm, the soul. It is then that prayer becomes most urgent and intense. It was said of Luther that he prayed "with as much reverence as if he were praying to God, and with as much boldness as if he had been speaking to a friend." One remarked of the prayers of Guthrie of Fenwick that "every word would fill a corn measure." Livingstone reports of Robert Bruce that in prayer "every sentence was like a strong bolt shot up to heaven." The biographer of Richard Baxter tells us that when he gathered his spirit together to pray, it "took wing for heaven." And it is related in similar terms of Archbishop Leighton that "his manner of praying was so earnest and importunate as

---

5. "It was seven years before William Carey baptized his first convert in India; it was seven years before Judson won his first disciple in Burma; Morrison toiled seven years before the first Chinaman was brought to Christ; Moffat declares that he waited seven years to see the first evident moving of the Holy Spirit upon his Bechuanas of Africa; Henry Richards wrought seven years on the Congo before the first convert was gained at Banza Manteka." –A. J. Gordon, *The Holy Spirit in Missions*, 139-140

proved that his soul mounted up to God in the flame of his own aspirations." Henry Martyn notes in his diary that, having set apart a day for fasting and humiliation, he began to pray for the establishment of the Divine kingdom upon earth, with particular mention of India. He received so great an enlargement, and had such energy and delight in prayer, as he had never before experienced. He adds, "My whole soul wrestled with God. I knew not how to leave off crying to Him to fulfill His promises, chiefly pleading His own glorious power."

How much of the regeneration of Central Africa do we not owe to the prayers of David Livingstone? He did not live to see the healing of "the open sore"; it was not given to him to know the advancing Christian culture of "the dark continent." But the record of his prayers is on high. His journals give some slight indication of his lonely vigils, his daily and nightly intercessions. He lived praying for Africa, and when he felt the coldness of death seizing upon his frame, he crept out of bed, and as he knelt upon the floor of the rude grass hut in Chitambo's village in Ilala, his soul took flight to God in prayer. He died, his sympathetic biographer informs us, "in the act of praying prayer offered in that reverential attitude about which he was always so particular; commending his own spirit, with all his dear ones, as was his wont, into the hands of his Saviour, and commending Africa—his own dear Africa—with all her woes, and sins, and wrongs, to the Avenger of the oppressed and the Redeemer of the lost."

Prayer is the means by which we obtain all the graces which rain down upon us from the Divine Fountain of Goodness and Love.

–Laurence Scupoli

There was a poor widow woman in that countryside, as I came through, that was worth many of you. She was asked, How she did in this evil time? I do very well, says she; I get more of one verse of the Bible now than I did of it all langsyne. He hath cast me the keys of the pantry-door, and bidden me take my fill.

–Alexander Peden

The consolation of Scriptures consisteth in this, that reading in them the promises of God, we do anew confirm, and fortify ourselves in Hope; there promising unto us that which betides to one to whom a Lord promiseth by his Letters a thousand Duckets of income, who maintains himself in the Hope to have that revenew through patience, fortifying his heart more and more through hope, when it seems to him that the accomplishment of the promise is delayed, no waies departing from his hope, and comforting himself with the Letter of the Lord.

–Juan de Valdés (Nicholas Ferrar's Translation)

CHAPTER 7

The Hidden Riches of the Secret Place

In the Revised Version of the New Testament, the ear misses the familiar ending of the text which in these pages we have kept before us. Instead of the words "shall reward thee openly," we now read, "shall recompense thee" (Matt. 6:6). The return of prayer is, in the first instance, personal and private; it is "the hidden riches" of the secret place (Isa. 45:3). Then, as it passes out into life and action, it is made manifest. The Father who is in secret, and who seeth in secret, rewards His servants "openly."

1. HOLINESS

In Bunyan's *Pilgrim's Progress*, we read that when the Pilgrims had come almost to the end of the enchanted ground, "they perceived that a little before them was a solemn noise, as of one that was much concerned. So they went on, and looked before them; and, behold, they saw, as they thought, a man upon his knees, with his hands and eyes lifted up, and speaking, as they thought, earnestly to one that was above. They drew nigh, but could not tell what he said; so they went softly till he had done. When he had done, he got up, and began to run towards the Celestial City."

This is the first reward of the secret place; through prayer our graces are quickened, and holiness is wrought in us. "Holiness," says Hewitson, "is a habit of mind—a setting of the Lord continually before one's eyes, a constant walking with God as one with whom we are agreed." And in the attainment and maintenance of unbroken communion, "Prayer is amongst duties, as faith is amongst graces." Richard Sibbes reminds us that "Prayer exercises all the graces of the Spirit," and Flavel confirms the sentence: "You must strive," he writes, "to excel in this, forasmuch as no grace within or service without can thrive without it." Berridge affirms that "all decays begin in the closet; no heart thrives without much secret converse with God, and nothing will make amends for the want of it." On the other hand, he acknowledges, "I never rose from secret prayer without some quickening. Even when I set about it with heaviness or reluctance the Lord is pleased in mercy to meet me in it." Similarly, Fraser of Brea declares, "I find myself better and worse as I decay and increase in prayer."

If prayer is hindered, even though it be hindered by devotion to other duties of religion, the health of the soul is impaired. Henry Martyn laments in his diary that "want of private devotional reading and shortness of prayer, through incessant sermon-making, had produced much strangeness" between God and his soul. Communion with God is the condition of spiritual growth. It is the soil in which all the graces of the divine life root themselves. If the virtues were the work of man, we might perfect them one by one, but they are "the fruit of the Spirit" (Gal. 5:22-23), and grow together in one common life. When Philip Saphir embraced Christianity, he said, "I have found a religion for my whole nature." Holiness is the harmonious perfection, the "wholeness" of the soul.

While we abide in Christ, we ought not to allow ourselves to be discouraged by the apparent slowness of our advancement in grace. In nature, growth proceeds with varying speed. Sibbes compares the progressive sanctification of believers to "the increase in herbs and trees," which "grow at the root in winter, in the leaf in summer, and in the seed in autumn." The first of these forms of increase seems very slow; the second is more rapid; the third rushes on to full maturity. In a few days of early autumn, a field of grain will seem to ripen more than in weeks of midsummer.

2. Intimacy with Christ

Communion with God discovers the excellence of His character, and by beholding Him the soul is transformed. Holiness is conformity to Christ, and this is secured by a growing intimacy with Him. It is evident that this consideration opens up a vast field for reflection. We shall merely indicate one or two of the many directions in which it applies.

(a) And first, the habit of prayerfulness produces a singular *serenity of spirit*. To use Bengel's phrase, we are "built up into a recollected consciousness of God."

When one looks into the quiet eyes of Him that sitteth upon the throne, the tremors of the spirit are stilled. Pharaoh, king of Egypt, is but a noise; and the valley of the shadow of death is tuneful with songs of praise. Storms may rave beneath our feet, but the sky above is blue. We take our station with Christ in heavenly places; we dwell in the Sabbath of God. "Here I lie," said Thomas Halyburton when his death-hour was drawing near, "pained without pain, without strength yet strong." Seguier, a French Protestant, who was sentenced to death, was mockingly asked by one of his guards how he felt. He replied, "My soul is as a garden, full of shelter and fountains." There are towns in Europe which would be almost insupportably hot in midsummer were it not that rivers, issuing from the ice-fields of Switzerland, diffuse a cool and refreshing air even in the sultry noon. And so the river of the water of life, which flows from under the throne of God and the Lamb, makes glad the city of God (Rev. 22:1; Ps. 46:4). "Prayer is the peace of our spirits, the stillness of our thoughts, the evenness of our recollection, the seat of our meditation, the rest of our cares, and the calm of our tempest."[1]

(b) Again, those who continually exercise themselves in prayer are taught

---

1. Jeremy Taylor, *The Return of Prayers*. This applies also on a lower level. George Müller writes, "These last three days I have had very little real communion with God, and have therefore been very weak spiritually, and have several times felt irritability of temper. May God in mercy help me to have more secret prayer." –*Autobiography*, 67.

to *rule their lives according to the will of God*. This effect follows naturally upon the former, for "all noble, moral energy roots itself in moral calm."

Prayer is the avowal of our creature-dependence. For the believer also it is the acknowledgment that he is not his own, but is, by reason of the great atonement, the "purchased possession" of the Son of God (Eph. 1:14). Pius IV, hearing of Calvin's death, exclaimed: "Ah, the strength of that proud heretic lay in this, that riches and honour were nothing to him." David Livingstone, in the heart of darkest Africa, writes in his Journal, "My Jesus, my King, my Life, my All, I again dedicate my whole self to Thee." Bengel spoke in the name of all the children of faith when he said, "All I am, and have, both in principle and practice, is to be summed up in this one expression—the Lord's property. My belonging totally to Christ as my Saviour is all my salvation and all my desire. I have no other glory than this, and I want no other." Afterward, when death drew near, the following words were pronounced over him: "Lord Jesus, to Thee I live, to Thee I suffer, to Thee I die. Thine I am in death and in life; save and bless me, O Saviour, for ever and ever. Amen." At the words "Thine I am," he laid his right hand upon his heart, in token of his full and hearty assent. And so he fell asleep in Jesus.

Such is the normal attitude of the redeemed soul, an attitude which prayer acknowledges and confirms.

Further, in prayer we present ourselves to God, holding our motives in His clear light, and estimating them after the counsel of His will. Thus our thoughts and feelings arrange themselves into classes (as in a process of polishing or smoothing); those that rise toward the honour of God taking precedence of those that drift downward toward the gratification of self. And so the great decisions of life are prepared. In prayer, Jacob became Israel; in prayer, Daniel saw Christ's day, and was glad; in prayer, Saul of Tarsus received his commission to go "far hence" among the Gentiles; in prayer, the Son of Man accomplished His obedience and embraced His cross. It does not always happen, however, that the cardinal points of life are recognized in the very place and hour of prayer. Helmholtz, the celebrated physicist, used to say that his greatest discoveries came to him, not in the laboratory, but when he was walking, perhaps along a country road, in perfect freedom of mind. But his discoveries merely registered themselves then; they were really brought to the birth in the laboratory. And whether it be in the place of prayer, or elsewhere, that life's great decisions frame themselves, undoubtedly it is in the silent hour that characters are molded and careers determined.

In his Autobiography George Müller gives a striking testimony: "I never remember, in all my Christian course, a period now (in March, 1895) of sixty-nine years and four months, that I ever SINCERELY and PATIENTLY sought to know the will of God by the teaching of the Holy Ghost, through the instrumentality of the Word of God, but I have been ALWAYS directed rightly. But if honesty of heart and uprightness before God were lacking, or if I did not patiently wait before God for instruction, or if I preferred the counsel of my fellow-men to the declarations of the Word of the Living God, I made great mistakes." As we present ourselves before the Lord in prayer, we open our hearts to the Holy Spirit when we yield to the inward impulse, and the Divine energy commands our being. Our plans, if we have formed them at the dictation of nature, are laid aside, and the purpose of God in relation to our lives is accepted. As we are Spirit-born, let us be Spirit-controlled: "If we live in the Spirit, let us also walk in the Spirit" (Gal. 5:25).

(c) Through the acceptance of the will of God for us, we are led out into a richer influence and a *wider usefulness*.

Montalembert once complained to Lacordaire, "How little it is that man can do for his fellows! Of all his miseries this is the greatest." It is true that we can effect little for one another by ordinary human means, but much may be done by prayer.

> More things are wrought by prayer
> Than this world dreams of.

Prayer brings the Divine omnipotence into the occasions of life. We ask, and receive; and our joy is full.

An English scholar has told us that those who have helped him most were not learned divines nor eloquent preachers, but holy men and women who walked with God and who revealed unconsciously the unadorned goodness which the blessed Spirit had wrought in them. Those saintly persons had looked on Christ until they were changed into His likeness; they had tarried on the Mount of God until the uncreated glory shone upon their brow. Tradition affirms that Columbia the Celtic missionary, Ruysbroek the recluse of Groenendaal, John Welsh of Ayr, and many others, were wrapped in a soft and tempered radiance as they prayed. Such legends, no doubt, were created by the remembrance of lives that had been transfigured.

> I saw a Saint. How canst thou tell that he
> > Thou sawest was a Saint?
> I saw one like to Christ so luminously
> > By patient deeds of love, his mortal taint
> Seemed made his groundwork for humility.

But a changed life is not the only gift which God bestows upon us when we stand in the unseen presence. When Moses came from the Mount he was, as it were, transfigured in the eyes of the children of Israel; but he also bore in his hands the tables of testimony—the pledges of that covenant, ordered and sure, which had been sealed to him for them. His prayer had saved the people of election, and the law-tablets were the sign. John Nelson, hearing one comparing John Wesley, unfavorably, with a pulpit celebrity of the time, replied, "But he has not tarried in the Upper Room as John Wesley has done." It is this tarrying in the Upper Room that secures the enduement of power. But this line of thought leads out into the theme of our closing chapter.

Jesus, Lord God from all eternity,
Whom love of us brought down to shame,
I plead Thy life with Thee,
I plead Thy death, I plead Thy name.
Jesus, Lord God of every living soul,
Thy love exceeds its uttered fame,
Thy will can make us whole,
I plead Thyself. I plead Thy name.

–Christina Rossetti

None can believe how powerful prayer is, and what it is able to effect, but those who have learned it by experience. It is a great matter when in extreme need to take hold on prayer. I know, whenever I have prayed earnestly that I have been amply heard, and have obtained more than I prayed for. God indeed sometimes delayed, but at last He came.

–Martin Luther

I sought Him in my hour of need;
(Lord God now hear my prayer!)
For death He gave me life indeed,
And comfort for despair.
For this my thanks shall endless be,
Oh thank Him, thank Him now with me,
Give to our God the glory!

–J. J. Schutz

CHAPTER 8

The Open Recompense

In their anxiety to magnify the personal benefits which are derived from communion with God, the Greek fathers used to employ the figure of a boat moored to a ship. If one were to draw upon the rope, they said, the ship would remain unmoved, but the boat would at once respond to the pull. Apparently they forgot, or did not know, that in mechanics "action and reaction are equal and opposite"; as great an effect would take place on the larger vessel as on the smaller, although the greater bulk of the ship would make the displacement much less obvious with regard to it than as it affected the boat. In prayer also, the influence is reciprocal. There is, as we have seen, a heightened exercise of all the Christian graces; but there are also direct answers to petitions offered in faith.

1. Persisting in Prayer with Expectation

If we do not expect to receive answers to our requests, our whole conception of prayer is at fault. "None ask in earnest," says Trail, "but they will try how they speed. There is no surer and plainer mark of trifling in prayer than when men are careless what they get by prayer." And to the same effect Richard Sibbes writes: "We should watch daily, continue instant in prayer; strengthen our supplications with arguments from God's Word and promises; and mark how our prayers speed. When we shoot an arrow we look to its fall; when we send a ship to sea we look for its return; and when we sow we look for an harvest. . . . It is atheism to pray and not to wait in hope. A sincere Christian will pray, wait, strengthen his heart with the promises, and never leave praying and looking up till God gives him a gracious answer."

And if the answer is delayed, we ought to ask ourselves if that which we desire is truly according to the will of God; and if we are satisfied that it is, we ought to continue "instant in prayer." Bengel gives his judgment that "a Christian should not leave off praying till his heavenly Father give him leave, by permitting him to obtain something." And George Müller drew encouragement from the fact that he had been enabled to persevere in prayer daily, during twenty-nine years, for a certain spiritual blessing long withheld: "At home and abroad, in this country and in foreign lands, in health and in sickness, however much occupied, I have been enabled, day by day, by God's help, to bring this matter before Him, and still I have not the full answer yet. Nevertheless, I look for it. I expect it confidently. The very fact that day after day, and year after year, for twenty-nine years, the Lord has enabled me to continue patiently, believingly, to wait on Him for the blessing, still further encourages me to wait on; and so fully am I assured that God hears me about this matter, that I have often been enabled to praise Him beforehand for the full answer which I shall ultimately receive to my prayers on this subject."[1]

2. ACCORDING TO THE WILL OF GOD

We ought not to doubt that those prayers which are according to the will of God shall have a full answer, for with regard to them we rest our confidence on the Word and Name of Christ. But there are many requests concerning which we do not easily come to full assurance—they do not

---

1. On this point Müller says elsewhere, "It is not enough to begin to pray, nor to pray aright; nor is it enough to continue *for a time* to pray; but we must patiently, believingly, continue in prayer until we obtain an answer; and further we have not only to *continue* in prayer unto the end, but we have also to *believe* that God does hear us, and will answer our prayers. Most frequently we fail in *not continuing* in prayer until the blessing is obtained, and *in not expecting* the blessing." –*Autobiography*, 320

stand so clearly in the Divine will as to yield us certainty. And with regard to many of them, our prayers seem to return empty.

Moses desired to pass over Jordan with the tribes; but Jehovah said to him, "Speak no more unto Me of this matter" (Deut. 3:26). Paul besought the Lord thrice that the thorn which rankled in his flesh might be withdrawn, but the only response assured was, "My grace is sufficient for thee" (2 Cor. 12:9). John, the beloved disciple, encourages us to pray for the salvation of our brethren, but even as we address ourselves to this holy duty he reminds us that "there is a sin unto death," in the face of which, apparently, prayer will not prevail (1 John 5:16).

We may indeed be sure that "Whatsoever is good for God's children they shall have it; for all is theirs to help them towards heaven; therefore if poverty be good they shall have it; if disgrace or crosses be good they shall have them; for all is ours to promote our greatest prosperity."[2]

When we pray for temporal blessings, we are sometimes conscious of the special aid of the Spirit of intercession. This is, so far, a warrant to believe that our prayer is well-pleasing to God. But we must be careful not to confound the yearnings of nature with the promptings of the Spirit. Only those whose eye is single, and whose whole body, therefore, is full of light, can safely distinguish between the impulses of the flesh and of the Spirit.[3] Subject to

---

2. Richard Sibbes, *Divine Meditations*, 5.

3. The following extract from the *Life of John Howe* may serve to point a caution which has sometimes been too lightly heeded: "At that time [in the days of the English Commonwealth] an erroneous opinion, still cherished by some few pious people, respecting the efficacy of a special faith in prayer, pervaded the religious community. The idea was entertained that if a believer was led to seek a favor in prayer, such as the recovery or conversion of a child, or victory on the battlefield, with unusual fervor, and with the strong persuasion that the prayer would be favorably answered, such would certainly be the case. This notion was carried by some to still greater lengths of extravagancy, until it amounted to a virtual assertion of inspiration. The court of Cromwell was not unfavorable soil for the nourishment of a conceit like this; indeed, it appears to have taken deep hold of the mind of the Protector himself. Thoroughly convinced of its erroneous nature and unhallowed tendencies, and having listened to a sermon at Whitehall, the avowed design of which was to maintain and defend it, Howe felt himself bound in conscience to expose its absurdity when next he should preach before Cromwell. This he did. . . . Cromwell's brow furnished indications of his displeasure during the delivery of the discourse, and a certain coolness in

this caution, we may very often derive encouragement from the fervor of our petitions. John Livingstone made this note in his private papers: "After prayer, I am to look back and recapitulate what petitions God hath put in my mouth, and these I am to account as blessings promised, and to look for the performance." And Augustus Toplady speaks with even less reserve: "I can, to the best of my remembrance and belief, truly say that I never yet have had one promise, nor assurance, concerning temporal things, impressed upon me beforehand in a way of communion with God, which the event did not realize. I never, that I know of, knew it fail in any one single instance."[4]

3. WHAT WE SHOULD ASK FOR

What things should form the burden of our request? Maximus of Tyre declared that he would not ask the gods for anything but goodness, peace, and hope in death. But we Christians may ask our Father for all that we need. Only, let our desires be restrained, and our prayers unselfish. The personal petitions contained in the Lord's Prayer are very modest—daily bread, forgiveness, and deliverance from sin's power. Yet these comprise all things that pertain to life and godliness.

Bread and water, and a place of shelter among the munition of rocks, are assured to us. Garrison, and garrison fare![5] But we are not often reduced to

---

his manner afterwards, but the matter was never mentioned between them."

4. This "particular faith in prayer" sometimes engages itself in receiving the answer to prayers offered for spiritual interests. Speaking of the memorable revival in Kilsyth, of which the first fruits were seen on Tuesday, 23 July 1839—"a morning fixed from all eternity in Jehovah's counsel as an era in the history of redemption"—William Burns wrote, "I have since heard that some of the people of God in Kilsyth, who had been longing and wrestling for a time of refreshing from the Lord's presence, and who had, during much of the previous night, been travailing in birth for souls, came to the meeting, not only with the hope, but with well-nigh the certain anticipation of God's glorious appearing, from the impressions they had upon their own souls of Jehovah's approaching glory and majesty."

5. "Being asked by a lady if he would have bread and a glass of wine, he replied, 'If you please, I'll have bread and a glass of water.' 'Prison fare,' remarked the lady. 'No, garrison fare! He shall dwell on high: his place of defense shall be the munitions of rocks; bread shall be given him; his waters shall be sure.'" –John Duncan, *The Pulpit and Communion Table*, 37. See Isa. 33:16

such simplicity of supply: God is so much better than His word. He feeds us with food convenient; and if ever He should suffer us to hunger, it is only that our spiritual nature may be enriched.

But man does not live by bread alone. Health and comfort, the joys of home, and the pleasures of knowledge, are blessings which we may rightfully ask, and they will not be withheld unless our Father judges it best that we should be deprived of them. But if He should bar our repeated request, and refuse to receive our prayer, we must then reply with the First-born among many brethren, "Abba, Father, all things are possible unto Thee: howbeit, not what I will, but what Thou wilt" (Mark 14:36).[6] When we reach the end of our journey, if not before, we shall be able to say, "There hath not failed one word of all His good promise, which He promised" (1 Kings 8:56).

When we pray for spiritual blessings, we shall never ask in vain. James Gilmour writes to one who asked his counsel, "All I know about the process is just going to God and telling what I want, and asking to be allowed to have it. 'Seek, and ye shall find; ask, and ye shall receive.' I know no secret but this." And again, "You say you want reviving—go direct to Jesus, and ask it straight out, and you'll get it straight away. This revived state is not a thing you need to work yourself up into, or need others to help you to rise into, or need to come to England to have operated upon you. Jesus can effect it anywhere, and does effect it everywhere, whenever a man or woman, or men and women, ask it. 'Ask, and ye shall receive.' My dear brother, I have learned that the source of much blessing is just to go to Jesus, and tell Him what you need." A Scottish Covenanter reports that he received a greater increase of grace in one afternoon, spent in prayer, than during a year before. After two days' prayer in the woods of Anwoth, Samuel Rutherford received the white stone and the new name, to be "a graced minister of Jesus Christ." And how many, kneeling in an upper chamber, have received the heavenly baptism into "a sense of all conditions" and the witness of the tongue of fire? All the storehouses of God open at the voice of faith.

---

6. Mr. D. L. Moody used to say that he thanked God with all his heart that many of his most earnest prayers had not been granted.

4. ANSWERS TO PRAYER

It is probable that answers to prayer always bring their own token to the supplicant; but he may not always be able to convince others that the events which happen are due to the direct interposition of God. Let us take two examples, chosen almost at random.

"A Christian friend once sprang after his boy, who had fallen into the swollen flood of the Wupper; and as he sprang he cried, 'Lord, teach me to swim!' He swam skillfully, though he had never tried it before, and saved his child."[7]

"Once when a sudden and terrific hailstorm was pouring down upon the fields, and likely to occasion serious damage, a person rushed into Bengel's room and exclaimed: 'Alas, sir, everything will be destroyed; we shall lose all!' Bengel went composedly to the window, opened it, lifted up his hands to heaven, and said, 'Father, restrain it'; and the tempest actually abated from that moment."[8]

Often, however, the reward of prayer is so conspicuous that it is scarcely possible to ignore the connection between the petition and the answer. Let us take as an example of this the case of charitable institutions founded by their pious promoters on the promises of God.

The *Pietas Hallensis* is little else than an enumeration of deliverances granted to Dr. Francke in connection with the orphan-houses at Halle. Here is one: "Another time I stood in need of a great sum of money, insomuch that an hundred crowns would not have served the turn, and yet I saw not the least appearance how I might be supplied with an hundred groats. The steward came, and set forth the want we were in. I bade him come again after dinner, and I resolved to put up my prayers to the Lord for His assistance. When he came in again after dinner, I was still in the same want, and so appointed him to come in the evening. In the meantime a friend

---

7. F. W. Krummacher, *Autobiography* (Edin., 1869), 143.

8. J. C. F. Burk, *Memoir of J. A. Bengel* (Lond., 1837), 491-492.

of mine had come to see me, and with him I joined in prayers, and found myself much moved to praise and magnify the Lord for all His admirable dealings towards mankind, even from the beginning of the world, and the most remarkable instances came readily to my remembrance whilst I was praying. I was so elevated in praising and magnifying God, that I insisted only on that exercise of my present devotion, and found no inclination to put up many anxious petitions to be delivered of the present necessity. At length my friend taking his leave, I accompanied him to the door, where I found the steward waiting on one side for the money he wanted, and on the other a person who brought an hundred and fifty crowns for the support of the hospital."

The history of George Müller's Homes at Ashley Down is written vividly on the conscience of Christendom. Mr. Müller, among many trials to faith, encountered one which was especially sharp. Looking back to it in later years, he commemorates the Lord's deliverance and adds: "The only inconvenience that we had in this case was that our dinner was about half an hour later than usual. Such a thing, as far as I remember, scarcely ever occurred before, and has never occurred since."

William Quarrier balanced the accounts of the Homes at Bridge of Weir every month. If at any time it appeared probable that the balance would fall on the wrong side, he called his fellow-workers to prayer, and invariably the needed funds came in. Almost at the close of his life, he testified that he had never been in debt one hour.

"The God that answereth by orphanages," exclaimed C. H. Spurgeon, "let Him be God" (see 1 Kings 18:24).

5. Extension of the Kingdom

Less tangible, but not less obvious, are the answers granted to prayers for the extension of the Redeemer's kingdom upon earth. To illustrate this point suitably, it would be necessary to outline the history of the whole Church of Christ. One could almost wish that this were the beginning, and not the close, of this small volume. How the instances crowd upon the memory and stir the imagination!

By prayer a handful of "unlearned and ignorant men," hard-handed from the oar and the rudder, the mattock and the pruning-hook, "turned the world upside down" and spread the name of Christ beyond the limits of the Roman power (Acts 4:23-31).

By prayer the tent-maker of Tarsus won the dissolute Corinthians to purity and faith,[9] laid the enduring foundations of Western Christianity, and raised the name of Jesus high in the very palace of Nero.

The ruined cells on many barren islets in our Scottish seas remind us of the weeks and months of prayer and fasting by which the Celtic missionaries, in the space of one generation, won Caledonia for Christ.

The prayers of Luther and his colleagues sent the great truths of the Gospel flying across Europe as on the wings of angels.

The moorland and the mountains of Scotland are to this hour witnesses that "a fair meeting" between a covenanting Christ and a covenanted land were drawn on by the prayers of Welsh and Cargill, Guthrie and Blackadder, Peden and Cameron.

Before the great revival in Gallneukirchen broke out, Martin Boos spent hours and days, and often nights, in lonely agonies of intercession. Afterward, when he preached, his words were as flame, and the hearts of the people as grass.

A sermon preached in Clynnog, Caernarvonshire, by Robert Roberts, was the apparent cause of a widespread awakening in Wales. It is said that a hundred persons were savingly impressed by its delivery. Some days later, a friend of the preacher, John Williams, Dolyddelen, said, "Tell me, Roberts, where did you get that wonderful sermon?" "Come here, John," said Roberts, as he led him to a small parlor, and continued, "It was here I found that sermon you speak of—on the floor here, all night long, turning backward and forward, with my face sometimes on the earth."

---

9. "'The Church of God in Corinth,' a blessed and astounding paradox!" –Bengel

Ah! it is always so. Those who have turned many to righteousness have labored early and late with the weapon called "All-prayer."

Of Joseph Alleine, who "was infinitely and insatiably greedy of the conversion of souls," it is related: "At the time of his health, he did rise constantly at or before four of the clock.... From four till eight he spent in prayer, holy contemplation, and singing of psalms, in which he much delighted.... Sometimes he would suspend the routine of parochial engagements and devote whole days to these secret exercises, in order to which he would plan to be alone in some empty house, or else in some barren spot in the open valley."

Of William Grimshaw, the apostle of Yorkshire, it was said: "It was his custom to rise early in the morning—at five in the winter, and at four in the summer—that he might begin the day with God."

George Whitefield frequently spent whole nights in meditation and prayer and often rose from his bed in the night to intercede for perishing souls. He says: "Whole days and weeks have I spent prostrate on the ground in silent or vocal prayer."

The biographer of Payson observes that "prayer was pre-eminently the business of his life," and he himself used to strongly assert that he pitied that Christian who could not enter into the meaning of the words, "groanings which cannot be uttered" (Rom. 8:26). It is related of him that he "wore the hard wood boards into grooves where his knees pressed so often and so long."

In a word, every gracious work which has been accomplished within the kingdom of God has been begun, fostered, and consummated by prayer.

"What is the secret of this revival?" said one in 1905 to Evan Roberts. "There is no secret," was the reply, "It is only, 'Ask, and receive.'"

the PRAYER-LIFE *of* OUR LORD

"It behoved Him in all things to be made like unto His brethren,
that He might be a merciful and faithful High Priest
in things pertaining to God. . . ."
–Heb. 2:17

"Lord, teach us to pray. . . ."
–Luke 11:1

CHAPTER 1

Introduction

As prayer is the most exalted experience of which the mind of man is capable, so it is the least patient of analysis. The manner in which the Spirit of God acts upon the human spirit must ever remain a mystery. For ourselves, we have not made much progress in the exercise of prayer, if we are not acutely sensible of the insistence of desires so vast and formless that they fail to convey a distinct image to the mind: at such times our supplications express themselves only in groanings that cannot be uttered (Rom. 8:26). Nor shall we be able rightly to estimate the prayer-life of another, until we have first sounded the depths of his personality, our insight piercing to the dividing of soul and spirit. How impossible, then, must it be for us to speak worthily of our Saviour's intercession! The secret of His wondrous Person is treasured and safeguarded in His life of prayer, but it is revealed as yet only in part, for "no one knoweth the Son save the Father" (Matt. 11:27).

Our Lord entered into creaturehood and was manifested in the likeness of sinful flesh. He was born under law; He bowed with submission before the divine will. His spiritual life was nourished, as ours is, by the means of grace. As the Son of Man He preserved communion with the Father through prayer. We are privileged from time to time to overhear His priestly utterances before God; but we are rarely admitted into the oratory where His private requests were offered. Such joyous intimacy, such earnestness, such filial reverence as were displayed in those high communings with the Unseen, must far transcend our narrow experience. Never man prayed like this Man.

In one important particular, the prayers of the Lord were unlike those of other men. He who knew no sin, but always did the things that pleased the Father (2 Cor. 5:21; John 8:29), had no confession of unworthiness to offer to God. His was "the only conscience without a scar." There could, therefore, be no bar to communion with the Holy One, no distance required to be surmounted, no way of access had to be devised and secured. At the close of His earthly life, He lifted up to the Father for acceptance the full tale of His sinless years, saying, "I glorified Thee on the earth, having accomplished the work which Thou hast given Me to do. And now, O Father, glorify Thou Me with Thine own self" (John 17: 4-5).

The prayers of the Lord Jesus, though little is said of this in Scripture, must have been radiant with thanksgiving. Even in that dark hour when Capernaum, His own city, rejected Him, He rejoiced in the Holy Spirit, and said, "I thank Thee, O Father, Lord of heaven and earth, that Thou didst hide these things from the wise and understanding, and didst reveal them unto babes: yea, Father, for so it was well-pleasing in Thy sight" (Luke 10:21). His grateful devotion pierced the clouds, and poured forth under the blue heavens a song of adoring praise, sweeter than the hymns of angels. Even when He stood within one hour of Gethsemane's agony, within a day of Calvary's thick darkness, He testified to the buoyancy of His spirit: "Now I come to Thee; and these things I speak in the world, that they may have My joy fulfilled in themselves" (John 17:13). And the disciples understood; they knew that there was no happier man in Jerusalem that night than He who was thus anointed with the oil of gladness above His fellows (Heb. 1:9).

We cannot doubt that much of the Saviour's engagement with heaven in His hours of solitary prayer was in the communion of holy love with the Father. On the mountain-edge there was, we may believe, a nightly renewal of that fellowship which is beyond knowledge, an interchange of affection which the Incarnation had not weakened, though it had lessened its sweet immediacy. So that, mingling with the ineffable repose of the Son in the bosom of the Father, there ran the strain of eager longing which was to find its full expression in the High-Priestly Prayer: "And now, O Father, glorify Thou Me with Thine own self with the glory which I had with Thee before the world was. . . . for Thou lovedst Me before the foundation of the world" (John 17:5, 24). The Son of Man dwelt ever in the presence of God; and yet, in the days of His flesh, He yearned for that glad hour when, having completed His redemptive toil, He should ascend from His voluntary humiliation to the Uncreated Glory, and, bringing our manhood with Him, resume His Session in God.

We must not, however, suppose that the prayers of the Lord were only thanksgiving and adoration. He had many requests to offer, in supplication and intercession. He prayed for His disciples—for their escape from temptation (Luke 22:32), for the success of their labours (Luke 10:18), for their advancement in holiness and love (John 17:11). He prayed for those who were still strangers to His grace—the world of men (John 17:21, 23), the tribes of the House of Israel (Luke 10:2), the rebellious children of Jerusalem, to whom He had stretched out His hands, no man regarding (Luke 19:42; Matt. 23:37), the soldiers who pierced His hands and feet (Luke 23:34). And for Himself He prayed—for guidance in the crises of His life (Luke 6:12), for the continued supply of power in the prosecution of His ministry (Luke 11:1), for life to be granted at His word to Lazarus lying dead (John 11:41-42); that, if it were possible, the bitter cup might pass from Him (Matt. 26:39), or, failing this, that the will of His Father might be fully wrought (v. 42).

"I know that Thou hearest Me always," (John 11:42) said the Saviour at the tomb of Lazarus. All His prayers were answered. But it must be remembered that there were petitions which He refused to offer. In the ignominy of His arrest He said to Simon, "Thinkest thou that I cannot beseech my Father and He shall even now send Me more than twelve legions of angels? How then should the Scriptures be fulfilled, that thus it must be?" (Matt 26:53-54). He would not ask to be delivered from the hands of men. Not many days before, anticipation of the agony that was so soon to fall had forced from Him the cry, "Now is My soul troubled, and what shall I say? Shall I say, 'Father, save Me from this hour?' But for this cause came I unto this hour. Father, glorify Thy name" (John 12:27-28). He will not offer prayer except within the will of God. And so long as that will has not been fully revealed, His requests are tendered with submissiveness: "Not My will, but Thine, be done" (Luke 22:42).

His prayers were always heard, but the answer did not always come at once. God, it has been said, has His seasons and delays; even the Son must wait upon the divine wisdom. The Lord Jesus prayed that Israel might repent and turn to the Lord, but for two thousand years the Chosen Race has been wandering in the wilderness. He prayed that the nations should be given to Him for an inheritance and the uttermost parts of the earth to be His possession (Ps. 2:8), but to this hour "the whole world lieth in the evil one" (1 John 5:19). Nevertheless, it is written that the rejecters of the Messiah shall one day look on Him whom they have pierced, and mourn (Zech. 12:10). And for our sad, sin-cursed earth, the day is drawing near when the kingdom of the world shall become the kingdom of our Lord and of His Christ, and He shall reign for ever and ever (Rev. 11:15).

As we have indicated, those prayers of Christ which are referred to in the Gospels are for the most part concerned with His mediatorial work. The Surety claims for His people the fullness of the divine mercy; the Good Shepherd makes intercession for the flock which He is about to purchase with His blood.

Accordingly, so far as the record informs us, our Lord's engagements in prayer, with scarcely an exception, gather round that act of allegiance to the will of God by which the Redeemer bowed Himself under the curse, assuming our sin as His own. Let us note these instances among others: His Baptism, His Temptation, His Preparation for the Calling of the Twelve, His Supplication after the Feeding of the Five Thousand, the High-Priestly Prayer, the Agony in the Garden, and the Voices of His Passion. All these have Golgotha in view; they are the disclosure to us of what death meant to Christ. To the Saviour the mere article of dissolution could only prove to be the striking off of earthly fetters and the return to the Right Hand of power. Nor could the fierce aspect of the torturing cross terrify this Man, most fearless of all who have looked with unflinching eyes on pain. His royal spirit made Him in this, as in all else, more than conqueror. But the death that occupied His waking thoughts, and became the predominant theme of His supplications, until He came to "inhabit His passion," was such a death as no son of Adam had ever undergone. Countless millions have paid the debt to nature, but our blessed Lord *tasted death* for every man (Heb. 2:9). "It is Christ that died" (Rom. 8:34). The prayers of Jesus are written red in the blood of sacrifice. And so they reveal to us, as no other words have done, what the Cross signified to Him who passed His earthly life under its benign but awful shadow.

The writer of the Epistle to the Hebrews tells us that our Lord "learned obedience by the things which He suffered" and associates this discipline with the exercise of prayer: "He offered up prayers and supplications with strong crying and tears" (Heb 5:7-8). These words recall to our minds the agony in the Garden, but perhaps they have a wider reference. Not only upon Olivet, but often elsewhere, our Lord may have been plunged into anguish and amazement. On such occasions His refuge was the audience-chamber of God. And there, in the divine embrace, He became perfect through suffering (Heb 2:10; 5:8). In many of the Psalms and in the Prophetic Word, the sorrows of the saints seem to mirror the experience of the Master: "Out of the depths have I cried unto thee, O Lord. . . . I wait for the Lord, my soul doth wait, and in his word do I hope. My soul looketh for the Lord, more than the watchmen look for the morning" (Ps. 130:1, 5-6).

The intensity of the prayers of the Saviour was equalled only by the unconquerable faith in which they were presented to the Father. The word of encouragement to the ruler of the synagogue, "Fear not; only believe" (Mark 5:36), must often have been addressed to His own spirit. It was, no doubt, out of His own experience that He spoke, when He laid on His disciples the supreme condition of their acceptable approach to the Father:

Have faith in God. Verily I say unto you, Whosoever shall say unto this mountain, Be thou taken up, and cast into the sea; and shall not doubt in his heart, but shall believe that what he saith cometh to pass; he shall have it. Therefore I say unto you. All things whatsoever ye pray and ask for, believe that ye have received them, and ye shall have them. (Mark 11:22-24)

He confronted apparent disaster with undoubting heart; in desertion and forsakenness He comforted Himself with the thought: "The Father is with Me." He embraced the cross, pillowing His dying head upon the ordered covenant. His enemies, gathering round the tortured Son of God, bore witness to the most patent feature of His holy character: "He trusteth on God" (Matt 27:43). They marked that then, in that dread hour, His confidence in the Eternal Love was undimmed.

Ere His ministry drew to a close, our Lord antedated His passion and prepared to enter on that heavenly priesthood which had awaited Him from the first of time. "Father," He exclaims, "that which Thou hast given Me, I will that, where I am, they also may be with Me; that they may behold My glory, which Thou hast given Me: for Thou lovedst Me before the foundation of the world" (John 17:24). This is not the plea of suffering manhood; it is a request by One who holds the right of intervention on behalf of His tried and afflicted people. This heavenly ministry our High Priest shall exercise till the end of all the ages, for He liveth to make intercession for us. And His advocacy is for ever presented in the power of an accepted Sacrifice.

CHAPTER 2

The Holy Child

O ur Lord Jesus was nurtured in a home in which prayer was a habitual exercise. The spirit of devotion presided over all the household arrangements, and every duty of the day was jewelled with acts of worship. If it be true that

> Prayer is the simplest form of speech
>   That infant lips can try,

we shall not be able to date the beginning of our Lord's prayer-life. In His earliest childhood His mother would recite to Him many of the Hebrew Psalms, to this day the fountains of our purest devotion. Joseph would carefully impress upon Him the first and greatest precept of the law, "Thou shalt love the Lord thy God with all thine heart, and with all thy soul, and with all thy might," and love would certainly find expression in communion with the Beloved. As soon as the young Child had learned letters, the Sacred Writings were placed in His hand. As He bent over the parchments, heaven would open above Him, and He would be at rest in the home of God. We may be sure that in youth, as in later years, His every thought turned heavenward, His every word was spoken in the audience of the Father. There would also be with the boy Jesus, as with other Hebrew children, a cheerful observance of the ritual of the day; He would pass through ordered seasons of prayer, public and private.

We may let our imagination linger over the spiritual exercises of the

Holy Child, but where Scripture is silent we must refrain from speech. It is perhaps impossible for us to understand the unfolding of a spirit innocent of sin and supremely recipient of God.

The one flower plucked from the garden of that blameless childhood speaks to us of a tender intimacy existing between Jesus and His heavenly Father, and seems to imply a heightening of spiritual experience. That we are not too bold in suggesting this appears in the words written in the Gospel of the Infancy, probably by the mother's hand: "Jesus advanced in wisdom and stature, and in favour with God and men" (Luke 2:52). He had, with a devout humility, been anticipating His entrance on the full privileges of covenant sonship with Jehovah, the God of Israel. The emotions which stir the heart of a Christian youth, who is looking forward to his first public profession of faith at the Table of the Lord, may help us, if only in a limited measure, to understand the prayerful desire which filled the mind of Jesus as He addressed Himself to meet the solemn obligations that were imposed on one who should become a son of the law. Nor did He refuse to make a confidante of His mother. His filial remonstrance, when His mother breathlessly rebuked Him, leads us to infer that she ought to have remembered the sacred revealings of His heart disclosed to her in the Nazareth home, when the Passover festival was drawing night: "How is it that ye sought Me? Wist ye not that I must be in My Father's house?" (Luke 2:49).

Now we may think of the Youth whose schooldays are ended, and who has been apprenticed to the trade of carpenter and builder. He would join not only in the worship of the home, but also in the prayers of the synagogue, breathing into them, without doubt, a deeper meaning than that which lay in the mere letter of the word, as He supplicated Heaven's mercy, not only on His fellow-townsmen of Nazareth, but on all the people of Israel and on the Seventy Nations beyond.

During those years, our Lord acquired a remarkable familiarity with the ancient Scriptures. In the cottage of Joseph the carpenter—himself a son of David—there would probably be found some of the sacred scrolls:

Deuteronomy, the Psalms, Isaiah, perhaps, if we may draw any conclusion from the frequent appeal which the Lord Jesus made to these books. For some of the other Holy Writings, He may have been dependent on the synagogue chest. Nor can we think of His study of his Father's word—for such it was to him—without picturing to ourselves the continual uprising of His thoughts toward that Holy One whom the open scroll revealed. Our Lord's study of the Scriptures must have been inwrought, like some costly mosaic, with praise and adoration, petition and intercession. He would inlay every commandment in renewed consecration, every promise in heartfelt acceptance, every disclosure of the divine character in thanksgiving. Each separate word of God would be wrought by prayer into the framework of His life.

That there were special times of prayer, quiet hours of waiting upon God, when the youthful Carpenter of Nazareth withdrew from His fellows and from His tasks, and sought in solitude the face of His Father, we may be sure—not merely from our sense of what is fitting and needful, but also from our Lord's practice in the days of His ministry. Then, He continually sought the mountain silences. In Nazareth, He may often have climbed the hill that rises above the village, that He might be alone with God; more often, perhaps, He entered into the "closet," the little storeroom tucked in between the living- room and the workshop. Is there not a touch of reminiscence in these words: "Thou, when thou prayest, enter into thine inner chamber, and having shut thy door, pray to thy Father which is in secret, and thy Father, which seeth in secret, shall recompense thee" (Matt 6:6)?

It is good for us to remember this. A zealous labourer in the kingdom of God may say, "I am too busy to spend much time in prayer; and 'work,' you know, 'is prayer.'" Another, occupying a different standpoint, may profess, "I am praying all day long; I do not need to observe set seasons; my entire life is one of intercourse with Heaven." But we have not so learned Christ. No one was so careful to buy up the opportunity as He, no one maintained so heavenly a poise of spirit, yet the hours hastened while He prayed.

The experience of all saints is clear upon this, that we must carve out of the busiest day a quiet space in which we shall be silent before God. We must summon ourselves before the divine tribunal, permitting the light of God to stream in upon us, searching every motive, bringing every hidden thing to light, granting to us a fresh sense of pardon and acceptance, and revealing in new and ever more glorious aspects the divine holiness. So shall there be wrought in us the spirit of grace and of supplications. And God, even our own God, shall bless us.

CHAPTER 3

On the Threshold of His Ministry

From Malachi, until the advent of John the son of Zacharias, there were in Israel moralists and historians, psalmists and seers, but no prophet. For centuries men had been asking for an immediate utterance of God, but the voice of prophecy was silent.

John was in the deserts until the day of his showing unto Israel. We may suppose that, as he dwelt in his father's house in the hill country of Judea, the burden of the nation's guilt oppressed him. It was a time of spiritual darkness; the maxims of the age were worldly, and the practice of the people was ungodly. John fled from contamination as from a pestilence: he had "known pureness from a child," and the very touch of sin pained him. He left behind him the voices of earth, and in the solitary places of the desert prayed, "Speak, Lord; Thy servant heareth."

Then "the word of the Lord came unto John the son of Zacharias in the wilderness" (Luke 3:2). And with the word, power was given. He returned to the haunts of men, clad in the investiture of the Spirit. His message was that which had been spoken by the prophets of the olden time, soon to be caught up afresh and proclaimed by our Lord and His apostles: "Repent, and believe the Gospel" (Mark 1:15)—the eternal announcement of the divine mercy. "Then went out unto him Jerusalem, and all Judea, and all the region round about Jordan" (Matt. 3:5). Soldiers of Rome, tax-gatherers, vine-dressers, and fishermen—all the best in Israel, and all the worst, were there (Luke 3:10-14). Many of the Pharisees and Sadducees came in curiosity, but they did not submit to the baptism of John.

1. THE BAPTISM OF JESUS

Baptism was an ancient rite in Israel, and it had been employed in later years to seal the admission of Gentile proselytes to the household of promise. The new feature of this ceremony in the hands of John was that it was administered to Israel. A proselyte was said to be "newborn" when he submitted to the ordinance of baptism, so that in this rite John is saying to priest and scribe, "Ye must be born again" (John 3:7).

But if the official classes of religious Israelites refused to humble themselves in submission to the baptism of repentance, a Greater than they stooped to receive it: "Then cometh Jesus to the Jordan unto John, to be baptised of him" (Matt. 3:13). All the postulants for baptism, until now, had come confessing sin. Jesus came in the way of righteousness (cf. Matt 3:15). He had no sin to confess; why, then, did He take the place of a sinner?

In His incarnation He entered our nature, taking our liabilities upon Himself. Our Kinsman-Redeemer, He came to be our Surety and Substitute. And now, as He is set apart for His Messianic ministry, He joins himself to the communion of sinners, accepting baptism in waters that had borne away the guilt of an ungodly nation. In an act of humiliation, to be perfected only on the cross, He unites Himself with the fallen race.

This, in His covenant relation to His people.

Personally, however, His baptism was His self-consecration to the duties of the august service which He had undertaken: "Now it came to pass, when all the people were baptised, that Jesus also having been baptised and praying, the heaven was opened, and the Holy Ghost descended in a bodily form, as a dove, upon Him, and a voice came out of heaven, Thou art My beloved Son; in Thee I am well pleased" (Luke 3:21-22).

The decisive step has been taken, the ordinance which ratified the momentous transaction has been administered, and now Jesus gives Himself to prayer. In this prayer, as we may believe, all the motives and purposes which gather round the solemn act of His baptism find expression.

(a) He accepts the commission entrusted to Him. He arrays Himself in the mantle of the Messiah—Jesus is now the Christ. All the Scriptures have foretold His coming and declared His mighty acts. And not as the Christ only: He is proclaimed to be God's very Son. As in eternity He received from the Father a multitude of lost souls and engaged to die for them; so, in the inauguration of His earthly ministry, in human weakness and under the shadow of death, He renews the high, eternal covenant in God.

(b) He offers Himself as the propitiation for the sins of a lost world. The voice from the opened heavens, "This is My beloved Son, in Whom I am well pleased," is reminiscent of the Isaianic prophecy of the Servant of Jehovah (Isa. 42:1). For such an announcement there must have been a preparedness in the mind of Christ. The voice came out of heaven, but it was responded to in the depths of our Lord's consciousness. The Servant foretold was Israel's Messiah, predestined to suffer. It was of Him that the epitaph was inscribed by the Father, as on the rock-hewn tomb:

> He poured out His soul unto death,
> And was numbered with the transgressors:
> Yet He bare the sin of many,
> And maketh intercession for the transgressors.
>
> –Isa. 53:12

This Sufferer is now declared from heaven to be none other than Jesus the Nazarene, and the young Prophet of Galilee girds Himself for His passion. A path of thorns, with a cross at the end of the way, this our Lord in Jordan prayerfully enters upon.

(c) He asks for Himself a sufficiency of grace and strength—that He may have "an honourable through-bearing." Now the Spirit descends to dwell with the sinless One; the Lord of the house has come to His temple, saying,

"This is My rest for ever: here will I stay; for I have desired it." This advent of the Spirit, however, is only the completion of a uniting act prolonged over thirty years. Our Lord Jesus was Spirit-born (Luke 1:35), Spirit-taught (Isa. 11:2), Spirit-engraced (Isa. 61:1); from this hour, in an especial manner, He is Spirit-empowered.

The mystery of the descent of the Spirit upon the Son lies hidden in the depths of the Divine Nature; yet is partly revealed in the Incarnation of the Word, for the Spirit of God is the bond of union between the dual elements in the Person of Christ. But, as it behooved Him to be made in all things like unto His brethren (Heb. 2:17), we may gather from our narrow experience something of what the donation of the Spirit at Jordan must have meant to our Saviour.

A minister who is being inducted into the pastoral charge of a congregation, a missionary who is being set apart for foreign service, asks for, and by faith receives, the enduement of power from on high. The gifts bestowed are adequate to the necessities of the work entrusted to him. He puts on the robe of strength, even as our Lord has said (Luke 24:49). But the endowment which the Saviour craved was that sovereign gift of power which would enable Him to bear away the sins of the world, destroy the works of the devil, dethrone the evil one who had usurped dominion, make an end of sin, and open the gates of life to all who should believe. He asked, and all power in heaven and on earth was placed at His disposal. But the power came with (and in) the Spirit. By the Spirit He cast out devils (Matt. 12:28), by the Spirit He gave commandment unto the apostles whom He had chosen (Acts 1:2), and by the Eternal Spirit He offered Himself unto God as a "perfect redemption, propitiation, and satisfaction" for the sins of the whole world (Heb. 9:14).

2. THE TEMPTATION OF JESUS

In the story of the Temptation, related, one cannot doubt, by our Lord Himself, there is no mention of prayer. But the forty days' fast surely implies, and the parallelism of the temptation in the Wilderness with the agony in the Garden does at least suggest, that it was in a protracted season of supplication, which left a wanness as of death on our Lord's countenance (see John 1:29) and drew to Him a band of ministering angels, that the victory over the tempter was won.

The temptations which beset our Lord during the forty days of fasting are not recorded. But the triple assault which closed the series, and perhaps summed up the evil solicitations endured in this prolonged retreat, has been made known to us. The point of each of these last incitements of the tempter was that the Messiah should shun the predestined sorrow, and evade the way of the cross. "Master, pity Thyself."

(a) The first assault of this closing hour was an appeal to the principle of self-preservation: "If Thou be the Son of God, command that these stones become bread" (Matt. 4:3).

This is, in a more impellent form, the temptation before which our first parents fell. They were tempted in the Garden of delights, He in the Wilderness where wild beasts were His only companions.

They had all that heart could wish, except the right to partake of one seductive but deleterious fruit: He was faint with hunger and near to death. And with Him, as with them, the way for the entrance of temptation into the mind was prepared by the suggested doubt of the Father's love and truth. "If Thou be the Son of God." He has affirmed it, but is it true? And if true, where is the Father's care? Act independently. Provide for Thyself. Command these stones that they become bread.

Where exactly did the sinfulness of such a suggestion lie? It meant retraction of the Incarnation. He had entered into our nature, that He might live a holy life and die an atoning death in our proper manhood, living His life within the modes of our common humanity. It is true that He was God's co-essential Son, but it was not given Him to draw upon the resources of His divine nature. To draw upon them now would be to renounce His solidarity with the race.

And as His coming into our manhood was by the decree and council of God, to reverse the great humiliation of His entrance into manhood would be to disobey that holy will to which He was always subject, and (if that were possible) to introduce discord into the Being of God. The principle of our Lord's activity as the Incarnate Word is thus stated by Himself: "The Son can do nothing of Himself, but what He seeth the Father doing; for what things soever He doeth, these the Son also doeth in like manner" (John 5:19).

(b) The second assault of the evil one according to the report given in the First Gospel—and this appears to be the natural order—passes from the personal to the national, as the third passes from the national to the world-wide. "The devil taketh Him into the holy city; and he set Him on the pinnacle of the temple." If Thou be the Son of God, said he, cast Thyself down and angel hands shall bear Thee up. Dazzle the people into faith; give them a sign, that they may believe (Matt 4:5-6).

The essence of this temptation is that He should accommodate Himself to the prejudices of the multitude, the traditions of the scribes, the vested interests of the priests. We seem to note in the Gospels a willingness on the part of the rulers to acknowledge Jesus as a prophet and teacher, provided that He should compromise on those points which most closely affected them. That He should, for example, do nothing to interfere with those monopolies which had made the house of Annas almost incredibly wealthy; that He should accept the unwritten law of the rabbis as of binding authority; that He should be willing to become a mere miracle-worker, in order that the people might be impressed by spectacular displays of supernatural power.

"Cast Thyself down," said the tempter. It may be, as some have affirmed, that the Jews in our Lord's time cherished the belief that the Messiah was to be revealed to Israel in a way like to that which the devil proposed. If our Lord had flung Himself down, had been upborne by angel hands, and had stood by the great altar where the people were gathered for the morning sacrifice, it is possible that they would have acclaimed Him the Anointed of

God. But what would such faith be worth? There would be in it no sorrow for sin, no longing for holiness, no endeavour after new obedience. If later, on the mountain-side, He had received from the multitude who "craved for bread and nothing else" the crown and throne of David, what manner of royalty would this have been for Him who came to save His people from their sins? Or, again, if He had submitted to the subtle machinations of the priestly party, had infused into the nation a militant patriotism, and had precipitated a revolt against the might and majesty of Rome, how would this beseem Him who came to shed no blood but His own? "Move along the plane of least resistance," says the tempter; "use the tools that lie to Your hands; make the best of existing conditions; compromise." Jesus answers: "It is written, Thou shalt not tempt the Lord thy God."

(c) The third and last temptation goes out to the uttermost parts of the earth. These had been promised to the Messiah by the Father from of old. Now Satan assumes the right of governance, saying, in full view of the wealth and dominion of earth, "All these things will I give Thee, if Thou wilt fall down and worship me" (Matt. 4:9). If we think that this proposal is too outrageous to awaken anything but repulsion in the mind of the Master, let us remember that He Himself has stripped the glamour from this sin, revealing it to us in its native hideousness.

From the hill behind His home in Nazareth, our Lord would often look upon the ships of Tarshish, sailing out towards the Pillars of Hercules, or returning to Tyre and Sidon with precious consignments. He would watch the slow caravans coming from Mesopotamia, Sheba, and Damascus, and at times He would trace the march of Roman legionaries along the great north road. Already, in His boyhood, He had come to know something of the kingdoms of this world and their glory. And now, from this exceeding high mountain, He sees the flash of gold and the glitter of steel. He is made aware of exquisite harmonies and glorious artistic imaginings. He comes to know the craft of statesmanship, the advance of science, the range of philosophic thought. And Satan seems to say, "By these Thou shalt win the world." The force of the insolent demand that Jesus should recognize the suzerainty of the prince of evil lies, it may be, in the presumption that sin belongs to the nature of man, and may be expelled, nay, must be, by natural means. If, in the upward process of development, we have passed from the lowest forms of non-moral savagery, we must still proceed, it has been said, along that upward path, shedding the vestiges of a lower creation, and evolving righteousness and truth by persistent tracking of high ideals. But attractive as this scheme appears to many, it possesses two fatal flaws: it asserts that sin is native to the soul, and it denies the virtue of the Cross of Christ.

On the mountains of Quarantania, Jesus lifted up His eyes and saw the vision which Ezekiel had once beheld, which John the beloved was yet to see—"the frame of a city towards the south"; a city whose walls are salvation, whose gates are praise. Those gates are open continually, day and night, for there is no night there. And through the uplifted portals there streams a multitude that no man can number, arrayed in white robes, with palms in their hands, singing the new song of redeeming love, and pressing over the golden ways to the throne of God and the Lamb. And Jesus, turning from the tempter with the stern word, "Get thee behind Me, Satan," sets His face towards the hill of shame, still far away, but soon to be surmounted by a cross.

Chapter 4

All Prayer

S t. Paul mentions "all prayer" as one of the weapons in the armoury of God (Eph. 6:18). Our Lord, it need hardly be said, engaged in all manner of prayer.

1. Social and Public Intercession

We may contemplate Him first as sharing in social and public intercession.

(a) We think of Him as uniting in worship with all the children of faith, as it is written: "In the midst of the congregation will I sing praise unto Thee" (Heb. 2:12). At the opening of His ministry He proceeded, "as His custom was" to the Nazareth synagogue. Sabbath after Sabbath, He associated Himself in prayer and thanksgiving with all the men and women of good will who met there for worship. Afterward, in the temple and at the ritual feasts, He would certainly join in the services of the law. In His opening manhood, as the responsibilities of life were claiming His peculiar care, He reminded His parents of His duty as an Israelite: "Wist ye not that I must be in My Father's house?" (Luke 2:49). In His inaugural mission to Jerusalem He described the temple as a house of prayer for all nations. When, after His departure, His disciples were continually in the temple giving thanks to God, it is probable that they were to some extent influenced by their Master's example.

In one respect, as we have already said, His prayers would not be in unison with those of other worshippers—He knew no sin; He had no personal confession to present. Yet He was even then, in the eternal decree, bearing the guilt of men—Sin-bearer for the race. In His intercession He was already taking upon Himself our trespass; as the Mediator He accepted responsibility for the sins of the whole world.

(b) It is evident also that our Lord was accustomed to unite with His disciples in a common supplication. They and He, for example, would join in the "Thanksgiving for the breaking of bread" at the daily meal. On the mountain-side, according to His wont, He blessed the Giver of all good, as He took into His hands the meagre supplies that were to be increased to meet the needs of the many (John 6:11). At the Supper-table He, as Ruler of the Feast, "gave thanks" (Luke 22:17, 19). This act of worship may have been in addition to the form of words prescribed for use at the Passover. We may think of it as a fervent outpouring of spirit, as the Scottish paraphrase suggests:

> And after thanks and glory given
> To Him that rules in earth and heaven,
> That symbol of His flesh He broke,
> And thus to all His followers spoke.

The prayer which closed the Paschal celebration was, as we know, one that rose immeasurably above the ritual of the festival. It is recorded, for our admonition and strengthening in love, in the seventeenth chapter of the Gospel according to St. John. It is, if we may use the phrase, a high example of the "family worship" with which our Lord and His disciples were wont to close the day.

(c) But this prayer was, in addition, a priestly act. Although He was not of the lineage of Aaron, our Lord was, upon earth, one chosen from among men in things pertaining to God. As in Ephraim He had taken the little children in His arms, laying His hands on them as He made intercession on their behalf, so, in the valley of the Kidron, He blesses with uplifted hands the Church which He is about to purchase with His blood: "I pray for those whom Thou hast given Me . . . neither for these only do I pray, but for them also that believe on Me through their word . . . that the world may believe that thou didst send Me" (John 17). This is the only sustained prayer of Christ which has been given to us. As one has truly said: "We cannot thankfully enough wonder at and magnify the goodness of God, who has taken care that one of the prayers in which the Son of God poured out His heart to the Father should be so carefully communicated to us." As we listen to those words of our Covenant-Surety, it is as if a door were opened in heaven, and we beheld the Lamb in the midst of the throne.

The last act of our Saviour's ministry was in the power of an unchangeable priesthood: "He led them out until they were over against Bethany: and He lifted up His hands, and blessed them" (Luke 24:50). As He blessed them, He was parted from them, and was carried up into heaven. That unfinished blessing rests upon His Church today. The Amen will be uttered only on His return in the glory of the Father, apart from sin, unto salvation.

2. Solitary Communings

Let us speak next of His solitary communings. Sometimes He went forth to pray "a great while before day" (Mark 1:35), at other times He outwatched the stars (Matt. 14:25), once at least He spent the entire night in supplication (Luke 6:12).

> Cold mountains and the midnight air
> Witnessed the fervour of His prayer.

He had much to say to the Father, much to hear.

Each of the Evangelists commemorates the prayer-life of Jesus, but it is St. Luke who brings it before us in the fullest detail. The beloved physician may have learned something of the worth and power of prayer from St. Paul, his great-hearted travelling companion, who poured his life out in intercession, "night and day praying exceedingly" (1 Thess. 3:10). Because of that high example, St. Luke would be the more able to appreciate this aspect of the Lord's service on our behalf.

In Luke 5:16, we have a general statement which throws a vivid light on the daily practice of the Master: "And He withdrew Himself in the deserts, and prayed." It is not of one occasion, but of many, that the Evangelist speaks in this place. It was our Lord's habit to seek retirement for prayer; when He withdrew Himself from men, He was accustomed to press far into the uninhabited country—He was *in the deserts*. In this sentence the emphatic word is the pronoun "He." The surprise of the onlookers lay in this, that One so mighty, so richly endowed with spiritual power, should find it necessary for Himself to repair to the sources of strength, that there He might refresh His wearied spirit. To us the wonder is still greater—that He, the Prince of Life, the Eternal Word, the Only- begotten of the Father, should prostrate Himself in meekness before the throne of God, making entreaty for grace to help in every time of need. The only explanation to be given is that, in coming into manhood, He accepted life under those conditions to which our human nature has been subjected. He "came forth" from God, He "came down" among men, He "became poor" for our sakes (2 Cor. 8:9), He "emptied himself" of the dignities and splendours of Deity (Phil. 2:7).

Bordering on the Lake of Galilee there is a strip of uncultivated territory, termed "the mountain," a rough belt of untrimmed pasture-land, rising swiftly from the margin of the lake to the plateau above. Here our Lord often sought and found a sequestered spot, where He might hold uninterrupted communion with His Father.

The open air had a particular charm for Jesus. The intense simplicities of nature wrap the soul in silence, falling around one like the curtains of the sanctuary. In the glory of sunset, in the hush of a starlit evening, in the pallid pureness of the dawn, God seems to draw near: the clang of machinery no longer fills our ears; we hear His voice in the garden.

It is probable that our Lord, according to the Eastern mode (1 Sam. 1:13) was wont to offer prayer audibly. This is, I think, implied in Luke 11:1: "It came to pass, as He was praying in a certain place, that when He ceased, one of His disciples said unto Him, Lord, teach us to pray." The disciples, having drawn near, heard a solemn sound as of one praying: they stood, hushed in reverence, until He rose and joined them.

But there was a still deeper need for solitude in the hour of prayer. Prayer is our entrance into the secret place, where our Father seeth (Matt. 6:6).

Both by word and by example, the Lord Jesus impressed upon His disciples the importance of solitude in prayer. At one time He enters the tiny store-chamber and shuts the door (Matt. 6:6), at another He makes His way toward a solitary place (Mark 1:35); again, He ascends the hill-scarp (Mark 6:46) or the high mountain (Luke 9:28), and often He leaves the city behind Him and finds an oratory in the Olive Garden (Luke 22:39).

We have reason to believe that He frequently united in prayer with His disciples, but we read that often at such times He would withdraw from them. He called His disciples apart to Caesarea Philippi, to inform them that His rejection by the rulers of Israel had been determined on, and that His death was at hand; in that place they seem to have spent a week in prayerful retreat, yet even there He separated Himself from them: "It came to pass as He was praying alone, the disciples were with Him" (Luke 9:18)—alone, even then. And as they proceeded on the last journey to the City of the Great King, "They were in the way going up to Jerusalem, and Jesus was going before them; and they were amazed; and as they followed, they were afraid. And He took again the twelve, and began to tell them the things that were to happen unto Him" (Mark 10:32). Once more, on the night of His betrayal and arrest, after He had offered the High-Priestly prayer in the audience of His disciples, He withdrew from them. To the eight He said, "Sit ye here, while I go yonder and pray" (Matt. 26:36); then, leaving the favoured three, He went a little farther into the sombre wood (v. 39) and fell on His face and prayed.

It is difficult for many of the Lord's children to find privacy for prayer, and into such an experience He Himself has entered. In the days of His youth He was one of a large family, crowded into a little cottage. Amid the vicissitudes of His ministry He was in journeyings oft, lodging perhaps in the wayside khans. He was frequently the guest of those whose opportunities of offering a place for retirement in prayer were severely restricted; at other times His hosts were careless of His needs. But always He sought means for private prayer.

Instinctively, as well as in accordance with habit, we close our eyes when we pray. This attitude is the outward sign of inward recollection. We shut out from our view the world of sense, so that we may concentrate thought on that which is unseen and eternal. The intrusion of ordinary interests would confuse our mind, the presence of even our dearest friend would prevent the closing in upon us of the powers of the world to come. In abstraction from all that is created, we come to realise the essential things of the spirit.

3. Silent Prayer

In the silence God has much to say to us. He comes to search and try, to throw illumination into the dark places of our nature, to discover what of secret and undiscovered sin may be in us, to reveal to us His holiness, justice, and love, and to bring us into a rejoicing harmony with His thrice-blessed will.

In the presence of others the Saviour seems often to have been immersed in the prayer of silence.

When the woman of Canaan besought Him on behalf of her daughter, He answered her not a word (Matt. 15:23). It has been suggested that, as her request would have carried Him beyond His commission—"I am not sent but to the lost sheep of the house of Israel"—He "telegraphed home for instructions": hence His momentary silence.

When the man who was deaf and had an impediment in his speech was brought to Jesus, our Lord, looking up to heaven, sighed, and said, "*Ephphatha*". The look was prayer, the sigh also, then followed the word of power. The word so spoken rang in Simon's memory: he felt that no translation could worthily render it. In relating this incident to his catechumens, even to those whose familiar speech was Greek, he felt himself impelled to give the word precisely as Jesus uttered it. Accordingly, it stands in the original Aramaic in the Gospel which John Mark wrote under the guidance of Simon Peter (Mark 7:34).

When, on His return from Peraea, the Lord came to Bethany, His purpose was not only to comfort the sorrowing sisters, but to raise their brother from the dead. For power to effect this He prayed. We learn only incidentally of this silent supplication: when the Lord drew near to the sepulchre, He lifted up His eyes to heaven and said: "Father, I thank Thee that Thou heardest Me" (past tense, John 11:41). May we not believe that, as soon as the appeal to mercy reached His ears (11:3), there was a swift uplifting of His heart to the Father and an answering gift of power? His unspoken prayer has been accepted; and now there is open acknowledgement before the people.

When the seventy evangelists returned to Jesus and told Him of their spiritual successes, told Him also of the antagonisms which they had encountered, "He rejoiced in the Holy Spirit"; then broke forth in thanksgiving. In those words of praise He seems to refer to prayer offered for them during their absence: "I beheld Satan as lightning fallen from heaven" (Luke 10:17-24).

The Evangelists relate that on the morning of the second day of Passion Week our Lord, as He passed by, spoke to the barren fig tree, and immediately it withered away. Next morning the disciples drew His attention to the drooping leaves, and Jesus, taking the fruitless tree as His text, read them a lesson on prayer, earnest and believing. We may judge that His words of doom to the pretentious but barren fig tree were uttered after a silent communication had been addressed to His Father.

No mention is made of prayer in Mark 10:32, but we are constrained to think of it: "And they were in the way, going up to Jerusalem; and Jesus was going before them: and they were amazed; and they that followed were afraid." Our Lord is advancing, to meet and break the power of hell. All His faculties are concentrated on the work which His Father has given Him to do. His face is "set like a flint," He quickens His steps, the disciples fall behind, shaken to consternation, stung with fear. Was there not in the mind of our Lord on that crowded pilgrim way a prelude to the Gethsemane agony?

We cannot but believe that an incessant stream of prayer flowed upward from the heart of the Man of Sorrows during the course of His ministry. Again and again it breaks forth in arrow-flights of prayer and ejaculatory thanksgivings.

Indeed, we are certain that, in the nature of things, it must have been so. Our Lord is foreshown in the experiences of the saintly life commemorated in the Old Testament, as when it is said in the Psalter: "I am prayer" (Ps. 109:4), and in the Prophets: "He wakeneth morning by morning. He wakeneth mine ear to hear as they that are taught" (Isa. 1:4). In the Gospels this continual intercourse with the Father is plainly asserted in many passages: "Verily, verily, I say unto you, The Son can do nothing of Himself, but what He seeth the Father doing: for what things soever He doeth, these the Son doeth in like manner. . . . I can of Myself do nothing: as I hear, I judge. . . . I do nothing of Myself; but as the Father taught Me, I speak these things. . . . I speak the things which I have seen with My Father" (John 5:19, 30; 8:28, 38).

So undeviating was this fellowship of spirit between the Father and the Son that we read in one passage of "the Son of Man which is in heaven" (John 3:13). On earth He had nowhere to lay His head; His home was in heaven. More than once the Saviour speaks of Himself as having, during His earthly sojourn, His dwelling in the Presence-chamber of God: "If any man serve Me, let him follow Me; and where I am, there shall also My servant be. . . . I come again, and will receive you unto Myself; that where I am, there ye may be also. . . . Father, that which Thou hast given Me, I will that, where I am, they also may be with Me" (John 12:26; 14:3; 17:24).

CHAPTER 5

Before the Calling
of the Twelve

"And it came to pass in those days, that He went out into the mountain to pray; and He continued all night in prayer to God. And when it was day, He called His disciples; and He chose from them twelve, who also He named apostles" (Luke 6:12-13).

It is stated only once that Jesus continued all night in prayer. He may have spent other nights in intercession, but there is no report of His having done so. Our Lord's spirit was maintained in calmness. His life was strenuous from the first, it deepened in intensity, but it was without strain. His days were filled with laborious service, and His physical frame demanded rest in sleep. One may, therefore, estimate the importance of this occasion in the view of our Master, when, in preparation for the calling of the Twelve, He spent the night in prayer.

From among His followers He is to select twelve, who during His days on earth shall be eye-witnesses and ministers of the Word, and after His resurrection the heralds of His return. He is to choose a company of men, who, by their testimony and doctrine, shall lay the foundations of the spiritual temple—men of open-air life, quick to observe and honest to report, who will not construe history in terms of a cherished theory; men of uprightness, who will adorn the doctrine that they preach, who in all good conduct will demean themselves after the pattern of their Lord; men who will be so firmly convinced of the truth which they profess as to be willing to die for the vindication of it, who will love their Master more than life, and will seek first the interest of His Kingdom.

The duties that were to be laid on the apostles were: to testify to the facts of the Saviour's ministry, beginning from the baptism of John until the day that He was received up (see Acts 1:22); to create the apostolic tradition out of which the New Testament has grown; and to found on earth the Church which He has redeemed by His blood.

As we well know, almost all of those who were chosen were faithful men, whose hearts God had touched; they were unskilled in Jewish casuistry; they were not deeply versed in Scripture truth; in some degree, they were lacking in spiritual perception. But now they are about to enter the school of Christ, and there is no teacher like Him. He spent a great, perhaps the greater, part of His brief ministry in training them in knowledge and godly fear. At the first they were probably like ourselves –ordinary people—but they became the foundation pillars of the New Jerusalem. We may form some idea of the change which passed over them, as they followed Jesus in the way and hearkened to His word, by the transformation which we are able to observe in the case of two of those selected ones—Peter and John. When we compare what is written of them in the Gospels with that which we may read between the lines in their Epistles, we find that in the early days of discipleship Simon Peter is sometimes rude, blundering, quarrelsome, whereas as he nears the goal he is courteous, lowly, of fair and gentle speech. The beloved disciple, too, was impetuous, narrow of outlook, and stinted in charity—a veritable son of thunder (Mark 3:17); but he became, after Him who has no peer, the highest embodiment on earth of Christian love.

Those elements which Christ wrought to perfect nobleness were already present in the character of those disciples whom He was about to call to the apostolate. They were "His own"; He had begun a good work in them; and His prescient eye saw whereto it would tend. In prayer on the mountain He asks that those aptitudes and endowments which He discerns in them shall be brought to perfectness by the Spirit of holiness. It was as if He foresaw the course of their lives, through temptation, persecution, and distress; He gauged their peril, He detected the snares set for their feet by the great adversary, and He prayed for them, that they might not be turned out of the way, but be faithful until the end. Nor can we suppose that His intercession was arrested at the point where those faithful ones sealed their testimony in death. All down the ages their influence has gone, and wherever the fruit of their labour has been found, there the prayer of the Lord Jesus has preceded. This night of prayer must have besought and secured the welfare of the Church until, under the flaming skies and the rending heavens, the warrior service of the Bride shall cease.

"Judas Iscariot, who also betrayed him"; all the lists end with this sorrowful announcement. We naturally ask how it was that he should become one of the Twelve. Was not Jesus able to read the deep secrets of his character? Undoubtedly he was. St. John tells us, "Jesus knew from the beginning who they were that believed not, and who it was that should betray him" (John 6:44). Our Lord was not deceived. We may credit the tradition that Judas was at first most earnest, that of all the disciples he was the most convincing preacher and the most powerful exorcist. He soon forced his way to the front rank in the apostolic company; he was appointed to an office of trust; he seems to have aspired to the highest place. Many, no doubt, regarded him as the most promising of the Master's followers; others would hesitate, judging that a flame so fierce and heady might as quickly expire. But Jesus knew; He needed not any should testify of man, for He knew what was in man (John 2:25). Why, then, did He receive the traitor into the number of the elect?

Does not our Lord still act in this way? Does He not often accept a man on his own profession, that He may challenge him to make that profession good? Was there not afforded through that calling an opportunity of salvation to this dark-natured man? Robert McCheyne tells us that our Lord, in His tender and wistful forbearance to His treacherous follower, endeavoured to the last to "melt the betrayer". We may be sure that such patient efforts to restore the wanderer had never been lacking: but all was in vain. Intimate fellowship with the Redeemer might have opened a way of hope to this unhappy man; but now the Lord Himself is forced to lament: "What could I have done more than I have already done?"

We may, however, see another reason for the inclusion of Judas among the Twelve. The primary duty of the apostles was to bear witness to Christ. They lived with Him in the most perfect intimacy; in His relations with them there was no restraint. They saw more clearly than others His pure simplicity, the transparency of His perfect truth. They gazed on Him with eyes of love, and said: "He is holy, harmless, undefiled, separate from sinners." But that this interior testimony might be complete, it was necessary that it should be confirmed by one who did not love. After a time the interest which Judas may at first have found in Jesus gave place to a dull hatred, which deepened into a deadly malignity. But he, watching in the inner circle with keen eyes of malice, was able to see in his grievously wronged Master nothing but holiness and truth, until, with the heat of hell burning in his bones, Judas flung the base silver on the sanctuary floor, exclaiming: "I have sinned in that I have betrayed innocent blood" (Matt. 27:4).

All this would mingle in our Saviour's supplications in those dark hours upon that lonely hill.

CHAPTER 6

After the Feeding of the Five Thousand

The news of the death of the Baptist seems to have come to our Lord's ears shortly before the return of the Twelve from their first missionary journey (compare Matt. 14:13 with Mark 6:30-32). For the relief of His mind and theirs, and in order that He might hear more at leisure the report which the disciples had to give—"whatsoever they had done and whatsoever they had taught"—He proposed that they should cross the lake, to reach some sequestered spot where they might be free from intrusion. So they "went away in the boat to a desert place apart." The crowds, however, who were gathered in Capernaum, marked the boat's direction, and, running along the shore, "outwent them." When the little vessel drew to land, the beach was black with waiting forms—men, for the most part, though women and children were there also. It was the time of the Passover celebration (John 6:4), and all Israel was keeping holiday. As the day wore on to afternoon, and the multitudes still hung upon His lips, our Lord spread a table in the wilderness and fed the hungry with good things. An undesirable result followed: a simultaneous movement ran through the crowd—this should be their King (John 6:15). They would compel Him to receive at their hands the throne of His father David. Wages were meagre, taxes were weighty, food was dear; Jesus was one who could understand the lot of toiling men; He was able to sympathize with them in their arduous course; moreover, He was clothed with divine power. If only He were to consent to rule over them, life would become restful and glad, for He would remove the heavy burden and undo the yoke.

Jesus had once before been asked to receive a kingdom. That was offered by the tempter, and He had refused it, although crown and sceptre were His by covenant right. It was within His commission to preach glad tidings to the poor, to heal the broken-hearted, to proclaim release to the captives, and recovering of sight to the blind, to set at liberty them that were bound, to announce the year of the Lord's release (Luke 4:16-21). But the Cross stood full in view, and He refused to turn aside. The time of which the Psalmist said, "He shall judge the poor of the people, He shall save the children of the needy, and shall break in pieces the oppressor," would come in its appointed season, but His hour was not yet. Jesus therefore "constrained the disciples to enter into the boat, and to go before Him unto the other side, till He should send the multitudes away" (Matt. 14:22).

Evidently the multitudes were unwilling to depart, and our Lord had to put an unwonted pressure upon them; at last they yielded to His insistence, and reluctantly withdrew to their homes. From a worldly point of view this action of the Lord appeared to be disastrous. It quenched the enthusiasm of the crowd, so that, "from that time many of His disciples went back, and walked no more with Him" (John 6:66). St. Mark gives us the explanation: "They understood not concerning the loaves, but their heart was hardened" (Mark 6:52). It was a Passover festival over which the Lord had presided on the mountain-side, a feast upon the sacrifice. The breaking of the bread was anticipatory of His decease. As He afterward reminded them, they had been sacramentally eating His flesh and drinking His blood (John 6:51-58). The miracle of the loaves was an acted parable, designed to teach that every good gift received from Christ was offered by a hand that was pierced, was conveyed in the power of a life laid down.

When our Lord had sent the multitudes away, He went up into the mountain to pray (Mark 6:46). Meanwhile the disciples were rowing out into the storm at His word. As they bent over the oars, one at least marvelled at the Lord's absence: "It was now dark, and Jesus had not yet come to them" (John 6:17). He saw them, however, from His lofty station, in the fitful gleams of the moonlight, as the cloud-rack drifted past; He observed that they were "distressed in rowing"; at the critical juncture He came to them, walking upon the sea (Mark 6:48).

We may conjecture that our Lord's prayer was, on this occasion as so often, a renewed acceptance of His atoning death. As formerly, in the Wilderness of Judaea, as later, in the Garden of Gethsemane, He confronts the Cross. He embraces it, saying in the great words of a prophetic scripture: "Lo, I am come: in the roll of the book it is prescribed to Me: I delight to do Thy will, O My God; yea, Thy law is within My heart" (Ps. 40:7-8). And the Father seals Him for sacrifice—the Lamb of God, stooping down, lifting up, bearing, and carrying away the sin of the world. It would be an irreverence to try to conceive the manner in which His mind would deal with the situation presented to Him. We dare not speculate upon those aspects of His propitiatory sufferings which may have passed before His view in that lonely vigil. But we know that His prayer was heard, and that He emerged from the conflict more than conqueror. In lofty grandeur He passed out into the storm, exulting in spirit as He trod the foaming waves, their white crests firm as marble pillars under His feet. Probably some effulgence of the glory of God which had clothed Him in that hour of self-surrender still hung about Him as He drew near; for the disciples, imagining that they beheld a spirit, cried out in their alarm as He approached the little boat tossing in the waste of waters.

This incident, conveying to us, as it does, intimations of the mind of Christ, is charged with an ampler meaning than that which the text directly affords. We may read into it a revelation of the mystery of the Saviour's intercession. He has ascended the hill of God, and now advocates our cause before His Father. His Church is on the storm-vexed sea, under command to gain the farther shore: His disciples labour without intermission, but make no headway, for the winds are contrary. They are in the midst of the lake, the boat is filling, and is ready to sink. It is now dark, and Jesus has not yet come to them. But He sees and understands; every motion of the quivering vessel, every curl of the threatening waves, is clear to His view.

His followers are preserved in faithfulness, they are held in safety, by His prayers. At length—it is now the fourth watch of the night—the morning breaks over the unquiet deep: He comes. Vested in uncreated light, He seeks His own, swiftly hasting on His way through the rage of the tempest. The exhausted rowers receive Him gladly into the boat, and immediately they are at the haven whither they would be. The storm is past, the toil is over, the night is at an end: the Lord has come.

CHAPTER 7

On the Mountain of Vision

1. THE SUPREMACY OF CHRIST

Our Lord had left the territories ruled over by Herod Antipas, and had crossed into the tetrarchate of Philip (Matt. 16:13); partly, on account of the threatening attitude of the Herodians, but chiefly, we may suppose, that He might in seclusion have the opportunity of instructing His disciples as to the certainty and manner of His approaching death (Matt. 16:21). The Cross has come in sight; and it is needful that He should tell them plainly that "the Son of Man must be crucified." A week was spent in the neighbourhood of Caesarea, as in retreat—in prayer and conference.

On what was probably the evening of the seventh day (compare Matt. 17:1, Mark 9:2, and Luke 9:28), Jesus, along with three of His disciples—those who presumably were the most apt to understand the lessons which the Transfiguration was fitted to teach—began to ascend one of the spurs of "that goodly mountain" Hermon, which towers above the plain and dominates the landscape. It lay across the frontier of the Holy Land, for this revelation was not to be given to Israel only, but to the world. We can still trace the path they took; first, among the vineyards; afterwards through the corn-lands, and up among the olive-gardens to the groves of cypress and acacia. Beyond, the slopes were clothed with dense undergrowth, emitting fragrance from aromatic plants; higher still the black rock looked through the thinning vegetation, while the snow-crowned summit gleamed overhead. But this knot of wayfaring men was not making for the crest of the mountain; they sought some retired place of prayer, where they might be "apart, by themselves" (Matt. 17:2).

They came to this mountain oratory to pray (Luke 9:29), to pray about death, the death of the Prince of Life. Our Lord went up to embrace His Cross, and the disciples asked that they might enter into the fellowship of His sufferings. The prayers of the Chosen Three were soon over. They wrapped their heads in their mantles, and went to sleep (Luke 9:32). But the Lord prayed on. He was girding Himself for His death-conflict. He repeated, as the fringe of the desolating storm of judgment crept towards Him, the words which He had spoken from the Bosom of God in the eternal ages: "Lo, I come . . . I delight to do Thy will, O My God" (Ps. 40:7-8). In the volume of the Book, the roll of the divine decrees, before the foundation of the world, it had been prescribed to Him. And as He prayed, He was transfigured.

The sense of something strange occurrent, which so often startles a sleeper out of slumber, unsealed the heavy eyes of the disciples. For a moment they struggled with the torpor that had overpowered them, then "when they were awake, they saw."

They saw Jesus, transfigured before them. His form was as the light, His countenance was as the sun when it shineth in its strength. His glance was like lightning, and His homely, travel-stained garments became white and glistening, as the fine linen of the priestly vestments, or as moonlight upon snow. This was not such a glory as fell on the upturned face of Moses, when in the cleft of Sinai he gazed upon God (Exod. 34:29-35); nor was it like the angel brightness that shone as an aureole on Stephen's brow (Acts 6:15). These were from without; they were the reflection of the Uncreated Glory. But the transfiguration of the Saviour was from within; the indwelling Deity was irradiating the garment of flesh, which till now had veiled its splendour. It was the first open manifestation of the Christ as He truly is and eternally shall be. The disciple of love says, "We beheld His glory, glory as of the only begotten from the Father, full of grace and truth" (John 1:14). And Simon Peter adds, "We were eye-witnesses of His majesty" (1 Pet. 2:16). St. Paul, who was not himself an eye-witness, gives testimony to the recollection of the early Church, when he alludes to "the illumination of the knowledge of the glory of God in the face of Jesus Christ" (2 Cor. 4:6).

Moses and Elijah were seen standing beside the Lord (Matt. 17:3). "The power to recognise them was granted with the power to see them." Moses the lawgiver, and Elijah the reformer of Israel and first of the greater prophets, together with the Messiah, represent the full content of the divine revelation. Simon arranges these in one series; Christ is first of the three, it is true, but in the same rank; in Simon's view we have "Christ and other masters." "Master," said he, "it is a good thing that we are here; allow us to erect three booths of branches—one for Thee, and one for Moses, and one for Elijah" (Luke 9:33). Truly, he was bewildered, and knew not what to say. Love speaks out of the confusion: "One for Thee, and one for Moses, and one for Elijah." What of themselves? Either they do not think of themselves at all, and that is love's way; or, and this also is the manner of love, it did not occur to them to think of any other abiding-place than that which should receive their Lord. They would not acknowledge any other home, nor could they endure the thought of being separated from Him. Where He is, there we shall be also—this was the ineradicable conviction of their minds. A dying saint was asked about his hopes for heaven. "Where else can I go?" he replied. Where, indeed, can the true lover of Jesus be but with his Lord? For:

> This I do find:
>> We two are so joined,
>> He'll not be in glory, and leave me behind.

Yet when Simon classed the Lord with Moses and Elijah, even though he placed our Saviour first in the series, God interposed. The Cloud of the Glory descended; and when it passed, Moses and Elijah were no longer visible upon the Mount: the disciples "saw no man save Jesus only." And a voice from the Cloud, a voice like the sound of many waters, the peal of a trumpet, or the noise of mighty thunderings—"such a voice," exclaims Simon, as he recalls it (2 Pet. 1:17)—a voice of divine authority, proclaimed: "This is My beloved Son; hear Him" (Mark 9:7).

Christ outranks all classification; He outsoars all grandeur: He has a name that is above every name. As one of the Scots worthies was wont to repeat, "There is none like Christ; there is none but Christ." He is peerless and alone; there is no other with Him. Simon had been struggling towards this conception during the three years of his discipleship, but he had not yet attained to it. He had often differed in judgment from His Lord; he had at times treated Him with undue familiarity, even with disrespect. Yet at intervals it broke in upon his mind that Jesus of Nazareth was greater than He seemed. His stricken cry, "Depart from me, for I am a sinful man, O Lord" (Luke 5:8), and his tardy but deliberate decision, "Lord, to whom shall we go? Thou hast the words of eternal life" (John 6:6-8), prove this. Now he begins to learn that, in the most absolute sense, the Prophet of Galilee is God's only and well-beloved Son. This truth was too great, too illustrious, to be received in a moment. It evidenced itself insensibly like the dawn. The day began to lighten, a shaft of cold light stirred the eastern sky, pale gleams of saffron pierced the cloud-rack, the day-star trembled on the horizon; then swiftly came the rush of morning glory, and now—the sun is uprisen. In later years, Simon found no words in which he might worthily celebrate the praises of his Lord. This Jesus the Nazarene had received a name all names excelling; He had filled heaven with His glory and earth with His power; from His mediatorial throne He was ruling the ages and marshalling the circling years.

2. MOSES AND ELIJAH

In their earthly life, Moses and Elijah had seen Christ's day afar off. Moses stood by the altar reared under the crags of Sinai, and when he had sprinkled the people with the blood of sacrifice, he announced, "Behold, the blood of the covenant, which the Lord hath made with you concerning all these words" (Exod. 24:8). Elijah repaired the desecrated altar of Jehovah on Carmel, and invoked that Sacred Name, until the fire of God fell and consumed the offering (1 Kings 18:16-45). But both these fathers of the faith understood clearly that the blood of bulls and of goats could not take away sin (Heb. 10:4); therefore, they looked forward to one whose coming had been foretold—a Prince and a Saviour.

Moses died at the mouth of the Lord (Deut. 34:1-5), and Elijah was borne up to heaven in a whirlwind (2 Kings 2:11). In the Upper Sanctuary they had had for centuries communion with Him who is the Firstborn of all creation (Col. 1:15), the express Image of Jehovah's Person (Heb. 1:3). After protracted companionship with the pre-incarnate but already manifested Word, it has been permitted to them to return to earth, to hold converse with the Word made flesh.

When the Wilderness Journeyings were drawing to a close, Moses preferred one last request: "Let me go over, I pray Thee, and see the good land that is beyond Jordan, that goodly mountain, and Lebanon" (Deut. 3:25). His petition was not granted then: on the heights of Abarim he surveyed with undimmed eyes the Promised Land; then, God kissed him, and he slept (Deut 34:1-6). Now, however, after fourteen centuries, his prayer is granted; he actually stands upon the goodly mountain of his desire, and views the whole land of Immanuel in an ampler field of vision than that vouchsafed from Pisgah.

In the reaction which followed the triumphant vindication of Jehovah's sovereignty, Elijah fled to the desert of the fiery law (1 Kings 19:1-8). He vainly tried to find shelter under the spare branches and narrow leaves of a juniper bush, and prayed in stark despondency that he might die: "It is enough; now, O Lord, take away my life; for I am not better than my fathers." One has quaintly suggested that, as the prophet of fire rode royally into heaven, he looked down upon the desert shrub where, in the deep gloom of his spirit, he had called upon death.

To Moses and Elijah, therefore, death was not a novel experience, although it had, in the case of each, been swallowed up in victory.

An obscure phrase in the Epistle of Jude (v. 9) may be thought to imply that the body of Moses was raised "out of due time" that he might take part in this earthly ministry of consolation rendered to the Saviour. On the other hand, the body of Elijah's humiliation was "changed" as he went up into the glory of God. And as the transfiguration of our Lord is confessedly a symbol and pledge of His return and of our gathering together unto Him, Moses and Elijah may remind us of those who shall welcome the Redeemer as He comes to earth in His kingdom and power: "*The dead in Christ* shall rise first; then *we that are alive and remain* shall be caught up together with them in the clouds, to meet the Lord in the air: and so shall we ever be with the Lord" (1 Thess. 4:16-17).

Moses and Elijah "appeared in glory and spake of His decease which He was about to accomplish at Jerusalem" (Luke 9:31). The impression left on one's mind by the condensed report of this august interview is, that our Lord was the speaker, and that Moses and Elijah waited on His words for instruction. He explains to them matters relating to the mystery of atonement in a manner such as it had not been possible for them hitherto to understand.

The word translated "decease" is literally "exodus"; "He spake of the exodus which He was about to accomplish at Jerusalem."

The going forth of the Tribes from Egypt was not a defeat but a triumph. It had its origin in redemption—in the paschal sacrifice (Exodus 12). As soon as the blood was sprinkled before the threshold of the slave-huts in Goshen, the Hebrew serfs received from God their manumission. With loins girt and with staff in hand they gathered to the Passover Feast. On that night, much to be remembered, they left the house of bondage. In the power of the blood of sprinkling they were made the freemen of the Lord Almighty.

Moses and the tribes of Israel stood by the shore of the sea, sheeted with storm-drift under the fury of a "strong east wind." As the lawgiver stretched his rod over the tumult, the waters parted, and the ransomed of the Lord went through the flood on foot (Exod. 14:21-31). On the following day, as the sun poured its level rays across the now placid lake, gleaming like crystal dipped in flame, the happy people, radiant with thanksgiving, poured forth the song of Moses, the servant of God, and the song of the Lamb:

> Sing unto the Lord, for He hath triumphed gloriously:
> The horse and his rider hath He thrown into the sea.
> The Lord is my strength and song,
> And He is become my salvation;
> This is my God, and I will praise Him;
> My father's God, and I will exalt Him.
>
> –Exod. 15:1-2

Such were the sacred recollections in which the Saviour enshrined the Gospel of redeeming love, setting it forth in ancient phrase as by a parable.

In the power of His own blood He would go forth, the first-begotten from among the dead, the leader of the ransomed army, trampling upon tempestuous seas, and making His foot-steps a way to walk in. He has entered into covenant, to deliver from servitude to sin and introduce to a life of holiness a multitude that no man can number, redeemed out of every nation and kindred and people and tongue. This exodus He "was about to accomplish at Jerusalem."

3. The Significance of the Transfiguration to Christ

In taking the disciples with Him up into the mountain, He may have been impelled by a feeling akin to that which led Him to say at the enclosure of Gethsemane's garden, "Tarry ye here, and watch with Me" (Matt. 26:38). Our Lord was brave beyond all telling, but He was not stoically wrapped up in the pride of endurance. He craved the sympathetic fellowship of those whom He loved, and it belonged to His self-emptying here on earth that so few were able to understand His aims, and they only in the most restricted measure. A gifted writer has told of a brilliant function: people of high degree were present; the whole scene was redolent of satisfaction and enjoyment. On the wall above the gay throng there hung, among other paintings, one of the Saviour, thorn-crowned and blood-bedewed, treading the wine-vat. No one but the writer seemed to notice the picture, but as she observed it, she remembered the words: "I have trodden the wine-press *alone*" (Isa. 63:3).

> Alone, O Christ, yea, evermore alone,
> In that strange anguish, even when close to Thee
> Thy people press with tears.

But here, as later in Gethsemane, the attendant disciples were unable to enter into the mind of their Lord. Thus it is, too often, alas, with us: we fail to realise the sorrow of His dying, His hunger for the salvation of men, the joy of His finished work.

But this consideration just touches the fringe of our subject.

From the slopes of Hermon, as the morning was about to break, our Saviour might review the scenes of His ministry. Far off, the ridge above Nazareth rose into sight; nearer, the waters of the Lake of Galilee flashed in the light of stars; here and there a cluster of dwellings, or a white edge of winding road, indicated the scenes of His mighty works. Samaria, Peraea, Judaea, oft trodden by His patient feet, lay stretched before Him as in a map. In the distance, out of sight, Jerusalem sat enthroned upon her everlasting hills. One can imagine the strain of our Saviour's thoughts as His eye rested on those familiar places—how He would enfold each town and village separately in His prayer of intercession, until His emotion may have burst forth in cries like these: "Alas for thee, Chorazin, Bethsaida, Capernaum. Ye would not come unto Me, that ye might have life. O Jerusalem, Jerusalem, how often would I have gathered thee." All His ministry, now so near its close, is summarised in that night of prayer upon the Holy Hill.

And as He prayed He was transfigured. Perhaps it was not on this occasion only that such a transformation passed upon Him. After a night of prayer on the mountain-edge, where He had fed the thousands with the scanty store of a lad's wallet, He had walked, in singular elevation of spirit, across the storm-vexed lake; and when the disciples saw Him, they cried out for fear. In that prolonged season of prayer, Jesus had surrendered Himself anew to the call of the Cross, and had therefore been crowned with glory and honour. Again, at the gate of the Olive Garden, where He confronted the soldiers sent to arrest Him, there seems to have been a majesty in His bearing that was not of earth, so that even the legionaries of Rome, seasoned and tested men, were flung backward on the grass as by the blow of an unseen hand (John 18:6). Was it not the lingering glory of the acceptance of His passion that smote with terror the disciples in the one case, and in the other the soldiers?

It was as He prayed that His countenance was changed. At various times in our Lord's progress to the Cross the awful meaning of the agony that was before Him fell upon His spirit with ever-increasing force. On each occasion there was a pre-libation of the cup which His Father had given Him to drink. The decision made in eternity had been ratified on earth again and again, each time with a more adequate comprehension of what it meant to be guilt-bearer for the world. And each renewal of His covenant engagement with the Father on our behalf had to be striven for through travail and dismay. In this transfiguration glory there must have been a mingling of emotion—love and pity, heroism and endurance, joy and peace. All the blended hues of heaven's light shone on the countenance that was lifted up to heaven in prayer on the mountain-side.

If we ask further what the transfiguration may have meant to Christ, we may observe these points: His righteousness was approved, His probation was brought to a close, His sacrifice was sealed, His reward was assured.

(a) *The righteousness of Christ was approved.* The Father regards the stainless life of Jesus and is satisfied: "This is My beloved Son, in whom I am well pleased." There was no blemish in His radiant character, no flaw in His perfect obedience. The years of childhood, of labour, and of ministry pass in review before God, and there is no fault in them. Had it been otherwise, the Son of Man could not have been our Saviour. The redemption of the soul is precious, and man must let that alone for ever: neither can he by any means redeem his brother, or give to God a ransom for him. But this Man has never sinned; He is solitary and supreme. And on the ground of His stainless purity His sacrifice is accepted.

(b) *The probation of the Lord Jesus was complete.* It seems to be taught both in the Old Testament and in the New that man, if he had continued in innocence, would have been taken up into a spiritual existence, as those shall be who are alive and remain at the Coming of Christ. Our first parents, had they resisted temptation, would have been raised to a deathless state. But they sinned and fell, and death came by sin. Our Lord entered into the defeat and tragedy of our race.

> O loving wisdom of our God!
>> When all was sin and shame,
> A second Adam to the fight
>> And to the rescue came.

And now, on the testimony of the Father, the probation of the Messiah is finished. When He had brought in an everlasting righteousness, He went up into a high mountain and was transfigured. He received an abundant entrance into that state of spiritual being which they possess who stand in the Living Presence and gaze upon God. Heaven comes down to receive to itself this Heavenly One. The glorified saints of the ancient covenant are representatives of that great cloud of witnesses who surround the throne. The Shekinah-cloud rests on the hill; the Father utters His voice, as from the mercy-seat; Jesus of Nazareth, by right of His holy obedience, has entered into heaven. He has restored that which He had not taken away, He has magnified the law and made it honourable.

But He will not accept the glory due to Him. The distressed and demon-ridden world is under His feet. He will not enter heaven alone. He came to condemn sin, not merely by winning an unbroken triumph over it, but rather by accepting the doom incurred by sinful men and by tasting death in their stead. He drew back from the opening heavens, descending the mountain, that He might climb the cross. "He loved me, and gave Himself for me."

(c) *On the Mountain, the Lamb of God was sealed for sacrifice.* "This is My beloved Son, in whom I am well pleased"–thus spake the Voice from the Cloud, or, as St. Peter describes it, "the Voice out of Heaven" (2 Pet. 1:18). Our Lord was not merely an innocent victim, a spotless offering from the fields of earth: He was Jehovah's fellow. The word here rendered "beloved" has a very significant meaning in Greek. It indicates the love that is lavished upon an only child; thus it bears the meaning here of "sole-begotten," and reminds us of the Old Testament word: "Take now thy son, thine only son Isaac, whom thou lovest" (Gen 22:2). It is as if the Father were recalling the scene on Moriah, two thousand years before, when Abraham, the friend of God, saw Christ's day and was glad.

(d) Once more, our Lord looked out through the travail of His soul, and knew *that His reward was assured.* Moses and Elijah stood before Him as the earnest of His purchased possession. Behind them was a great company of the saints of the house of Israel clothed in white robes, lifting on high the palms of unending peace.

CHAPTER 8

Blessing the Children

After the raising of Lazarus the death-warrant of Christ was signed by the chief priests and the Pharisees (John 11:45-53). His hour was not yet come; accordingly, He retired to Ephraim, a mountain village on the edge of the desert, over-looking the Jordan valley and the Dead Sea. Here He seems to have passed several weeks, but the history of those weeks is one of the unwritten chapters of the Gospel (cf. John 20:30; 21:25); no incident relating to it has been preserved by any of the Evangelists. We feel the sacredness of the silence. Our Lord was girding Himself for His approaching warfare and suffering: He was dwelling in the secret of the Divine Presence, holding intimate communion with the Father concerning the decease which He was shortly to accomplish at Jerusalem.

Those days of retirement had apparently drawn to an end, and our Lord was about to descend into the pilgrim way, that He might proceed with the Galilean company toward Jerusalem, when the parents of some young children brought them to Jesus, that He might "touch them," as Mark and Luke have it, or, as we find it in the First Gospel, "that He should put His hands on them, and pray" (19:13-15).

We speak of the "mothers of Salem," but the word used here for those who brought their children to the Saviour is in the masculine; fathers as well as mothers crave for their little ones the benediction of the priestly hands of Christ. Among the Jews the father took an important share in the religious education of youth (cf. Deut. 6:6-9, 20-25, etc.). It was even customary for the parents of a little child to invite an illustrious rabbi, who might be passing near, to lay his hands on the young head in the name of Jehovah. The Aaronic blessing (Num. 6:22-27) would probably be repeated, often, no doubt, with tenderness and deep feeling, for there must have been some of the Jewish doctors of whom it might have been said, as was reported of Henry Venn, that he never saw a young face without yearning to impart a spiritual gift.

But the disciples forbade them. It does not appear that those who surrounded the Master wished to censure an act which may have seemed to savour of superstition; for they would remember her who said, "If I may but touch the hem of His garment, I shall be made whole" (Mark 5:28). Perhaps they wished to spare their Lord an intrusion which might not be welcomed; but they ought to have known that this was refreshment to Him, not labour. It has been suggested that the precise form of the expression in Luke 18:16—"Jesus called them unto Him"—implies that "it was a pleasure and a relief to Him to have children near Him." It is often so; little children may be a fortress for troubled men: "Out of the mouths of babes and sucklings hast Thou ordained strength . . . that Thou mightest still the enemy and the avenger" (Ps. 8:2).

Probably, however, the interference of the disciples was due to their spiritual dullness; they failed to realise the value of a child's soul. How greatly our Lord did prize this inestimable jewel is evident in the unwonted heat of His spirit, when He observed what they were about to do: He was "moved with indignation" (Mark 10:14). This expression is nowhere else used with reference to our Lord. The only time of which it is said that His righteous anger overflowed its accustomed barriers was when His followers endeavoured to hold back the little ones who were pressing toward Him.

This, I think, is what the narrative implies. May we not suppose that, during those quiet days spent in this highland village, the little ones had learned to trust the loving heart of the Saviour? And that now, as He is about to depart, they cluster round Him, to offer a farewell greeting? Of their own act and deed they are coming to Him, as to one whom they confide in and dearly love.

St. Matthew tells us that some, at least, of the parents who brought their children to Jesus desired Him to lay His hands upon them, *and pray*. As is His wont, the Saviour does even more than they ask: He takes them up into His arms, clasps them to His heart, and blesses them fervently. The word translated "blessed" conveys the idea of deep and tender feeling. It is often employed to denote a farewell salutation. Our Lord is going to Jerusalem, to die for these little ones; He folds them in His arms, presses them to His heart, and breathes upon them a blessing which ascends to God as prayer.

Sometimes, as we look upon the face of a little child, we are moved with compassion, as we reflect on the course of life that shall open before this young "pilgrim of eternity."

> O little feet! that such long years
> Must wander on through hopes and fears
> Must ache and bleed beneath your load;
> I, nearer to the wayside inn,
> Where toil shall cease and rest begin,
> Am weary thinking of your load.

Perhaps our Saviour, pausing in the village street to bless and intercede, saw, with more than a prophet's vision, the long uphillward path, sharp with stones and overgrown with mantling thorns, on which those baby feet would tread. And into His prayer would come the immeasurable tenderness of the love of God.

Those who brought their little ones to Jesus besought Him that He would pray for them. Such a request could not be denied. May we not then believe that this one of our Lord's prayers would be fully answered? There is a tradition—though one without authority—that one of those little ones whom Jesus blessed was Ignatius of Antioch, apostle and martyr. May we not believe that all those children are now gathered around the Lamb who is the Shepherd of the ransomed flock?

I wonder if ever the children
　　Who were blessed by the Master of old
Forgot He had made them His treasures,
　　The dear little lambs of His fold.

My heart cannot cherish the fancy
　　That ever those children went wrong,
And were lost from the peace and the shelter,
　　Shut out from the feast and the song.

To the day of grey hairs they remembered,
　　I think, how the hands that were riven
Were laid on their heads when Christ uttered,
　　"Of such is the kingdom of heaven."

Still godly parents are bringing their children to Jesus, and still the loving Saviour takes them up in His arms, lays His hands on them, and prays. Shall His prayer not be answered?

CHAPTER 9

In the School of Christ

O ur Lord gave His disciples many instructions regarding prayer; with the help of these we may discern some features which marked His own prayer-life.

1. VARIOUS TEACHINGS

Most impressive of all is His insistence on the closed door, which shuts in the solitary worshipper and shuts out the clamorous world. Of this we have spoken. Emphasis is also laid on the absence of ostentation in our religious exercises. Those who love to stand and pray in the synagogues and in the corners of the streets, that they may be seen of men, have in such recognition their sole reward. If one should resolve to fast in his supplications, let him anoint his head and wash his face, so as not to advertise his religious fervour (Matt. 6:5-18).

Our Lord goes on to say that prayer should be simple, direct, and, in ordinary cases, brief. Our Father knows what things we have need of; we do not have to persuade Him to listen to us by our much speaking (Matt. 6:5-8). This, I take it, is for the common strain of life. God is not far from any one of us; whenever we seek Him, He waits to be gracious. In general, therefore, we do not need to persist in vociferous entreaty, "battering the gates of heaven with storms of prayer." A very beautiful verse gives us knowledge of a better way: "All things whatsoever ye pray and ask for, believe that ye have received them, and ye shall have them" (Mark 11:24). As soon as the prayer of faith ascends to God, the springs of power are touched, and remedial processes begin to work. We cast our burden on the Lord, and we learn that even before we called He had taken thought for us.

It appears therefore, that calm, brief, and trustful supplications are appropriate to the common things of life and to the daily task. But when we pass out into wider regions of the spirit, prayer assumes new forms.

When the disciples asked their Master why they had failed to expel the demon from the afflicted lad at the foot of the Mount of Transfiguration, our Lord replied, "This kind can come forth by nothing save by prayer" (Mark 9:28-29). The familiar words, "and fasting," are omitted by the Revisers. But even in the abbreviated sentence there is a hint of the stern urgency of the prayer that prevails. If it is unnecessary to storm heaven, it may yet be needful to break in pieces the gates of hell. When we are summoned to contend with powers of darkness in heavenly places, we must "prevail to overcome." There is an earnestness which bathes itself in passion, uttering itself even with strong crying and tears. It labours and wrestles, and strengthens itself to endure through an agony of supplication. Such was the prayer that broke the silence of the Olive Garden on the night that ushered in the death of the Redeemer. Darkness as of dereliction veiled the soul of the Sufferer; sweat as of blood bedewed His face (Luke 22:44) and stained the trampled grass; but He came forth more than conqueror.

In two parables the Saviour teaches us that persistence such as will take no denial, but will press on even to "shamelessness," is necessary when we intercede for the life of another; whether it be the individual worker praying that the bread of God might be ministered to him for the sake of his friend who is out of the way (Luke 11:6), or the widowed Church pleading for her children who have been fraudulently deprived of their birthright (Luke 18:7-8).

The formula in such cases is "ask ... seek ... knock" (Matt. 7:7).

We read that on one occasion our Lord "in the morning, a great while before day, rose up and went out, and departed unto a desert place, and there prayed" (Mark 1:35). This was probably His daily usage. After a day prolonged until evening in teaching, healing, comforting, He rose early in the morning, that in undisturbed privacy He might hold communion with His Father. On this occasion He remained in His chosen solitude so long that "Simon and they that were with Him followed after Him." At the foot of "the mountain" the people, curious and eager, were pressing round our Lord's dwelling. When the disciples reached the mountain oratory, Jesus was still in prayer. They listened, hushed to reverent feeling. When He had ceased, they say, "Lord, teach us to pray, even as John also taught His disciples" (Luke 11:1). The Baptist had instructed his followers to repeat specified forms of address to God; Jesus had not done so. Now, at the request of Peter and his companions, He gives them the type and substance of all liturgies—the ordered series of petitions which we name "The Lord's Prayer" (Matt. 6:9-13; Luke 11:2-4).

The Saviour introduces this form of words with the injunction, "When ye pray, say, 'Our Father.'" God is the Father of those who seek Him with a true and humble heart, and all are brethren in the family of God. In those two words, "Our Father," we possess the key which unlocks the mystery of prayer. He knows what things we have need of before we ask Him (Matt. 6:8); it is His good pleasure to confer upon us every perfect gift (Matt. 7:11). As the Creator, who built the framework of the heavens and instituted the order of nature, He is able to do exceeding abundantly above all that we ask or think (Eph. 3:20), and He accepts responsibility for the maintenance and well-being of His children.

The construction of this prayer is extremely simple. Three great requests on behalf of the kingdom of God, three modest petitions for ourselves, are all that the Lord encourages us to present to the Father in heaven. For ourselves, daily bread, pardon continually renewed, grace to help in time of need—that is all. But for the kingdom these:

Hallowed be Thy name,
Thy kingdom come,
Thy will be done,
    as in heaven, so in earth.

The triumphant conclusion, so familiar to our lips, is not in the earliest manuscripts. It comes to us rather as the voice of worshippers than as the saying of the Master. It is the invocation by the Church of the holy name of Jesus: "For Thine is the kingdom, and the power, and the glory, for ever" (Matt. 6:13).

We may pass from the consideration of this form of prayer, for, though we call it by our Lord's name, it was spoken to His disciples.

The Master goes on to give an illustration of another mode of supplication. A liturgy must be supplemented by free request. No ritual form can fully express the agony of Spirit-taught intercession which strives to communicate itself in groanings that cannot be uttered (Rom. 8:26).

Our Lord then spoke a parable that breathes a quiet humour (Luke 11:5-8). A wayfarer forsakes the bridle-path which should lead him to his destination; he takes the wrong turning, and presently finds himself in an unfamiliar byway. He wanders on until the night begins to fall. Soon darkness arrests the steps of the belated traveller, who is now "out of his way" (v. 6, margin). As he stumbles on, a gleam of light shines before him. Presently he comes to a tiny hamlet that is wrapped in slumber. Only one light burns; all others are quenched. The traveller asks admission into the house where the host still watches. At once he is made welcome; whatever of hospitality this bare home can furnish is at his disposal; but there is no bread. The bread for the day has been consumed, the bread for tomorrow has not been baked. The master of the house cannot endure the thought that his guest should go fasting to bed. He hastily reviews the possibilities; he thinks of one neighbour on whose good will he may count. He goes to this one's house, arouses him, and *asks* for the loan of three cakes of bread. To his surprise, perhaps, he is refused: "Trouble me not; the door is now shut, and my children are with me in bed; I cannot rise and give thee." The answer is churlish, and its crude selfishness stirs the applicant. He has been asking hitherto now he begins to *seek.* He implores his friend in the name of common humanity to give this man, already faint with hunger, something to eat; he reminds him of the obligations of hospitality, and bids him reflect upon the disgrace which would attach to the village were it once known that bread to stay one's hunger had been denied. But the unkindly neighbour remains obdurate: he will not risk the sleepless hours that may fall upon the household if once the sleep of the children should be rudely broken. The applicant has been *asking* and *seeking,* now he begins to *knock.* He is prepared, he says, to beat the door in; then, infallibly, the children will be roused. At this the neighbour takes swift alarm; he implores his friend to desist; he rises quietly, hurries to the door, and more than satisfies the needs of the troubler of his home.

This churlish neighbour—such is the boldness of some of our Lord's parables—represents God. The point, however, is not that our Father is unwilling to give, but that certain blessings cannot be bestowed without some preparatory delay. The host of this belated traveller is a servant of God, who welcomes as a friend the man who has missed his way. He gives him shelter with cordial goodwill, and would give him that bread which cometh down out of heaven. But this he has not of himself; he must go forth to make request for it. The bread of life must be received as the gift of God. Reasons for the delay of our Father, who wills to grant our request, but who holds us waiting at His threshold, may not all lie level to our understanding. This one at least is obvious: God has no more precious gift to bestow on His children than that they should possess words of life whereby those for whom they labour and pray may be saved. He will not grant this high privilege to any who do not value it aright, who ask it indolently or selfishly. Such a prayer must purify itself (as a river is cleansed in its flow) before it can be accepted by the Father. There must be an intense, a selfless, and a spiritual longing for spiritual gifts.

Having uttered this parable, Christ adds a further lesson touching that prayer which craves the gifts of the Spirit (Luke 11:11-13). When we plead for these the answer generally comes in an unlooked-for way. We ask bread, the Father seems to offer us a stone; we request a fish, does He not send us a serpent? We desire an egg, and that which is given to us bites like a scorpion. Prayer for spiritual endowments will in the first resort bring us very low; we shall be abashed and humbled; we shall be brought to the dust of contrition. And it may be that which was dear to us as a right eye, profitable as a right hand, must be taken away. To ask for the fullness of the Spirit may prove itself a costly undertaking. But if we are willing to pay the price, the blessing shall be ours. "If ye then, being evil, know how to give good gifts unto your children, how much more shall your heavenly Father give the Holy Spirit to them that ask Him?" (Luke 11:13).

2. THE PRAYER OF THE PERSISTENT WIDOW

Our Lord spoke another parable, to this end, that men ought always to pray, and not to faint (Luke 18:1-8). The incident which He pictured was such as might easily occur in the East. A woman, left a widow, was oppressed by a powerful neighbour or kinsman. He appropriated the farm or vineyard, left by the deceased man to the care of his wife for behoof of his children. The widow appealed to the judge, but the defrauder had been beforehand with her. He had offered, as we may safely infer, a substantial bribe for a decision to be given in his favour; so that, when the widow came crying for justice, she was driven away from the place of judgment. But as often as she was ejected, so often she returned. Morning by morning she awaited the opening of the court, and was always the first to present her plea: "Justice, my lord, justice." This continued until the resolution of the judge began to weaken. He vociferates loudly, but it is mostly bravado; he speaks with a grimace of humour, but he feels deeply. He says, "I neither fear God, nor regard men." Methinks, he doth protest too much. His conscience is beginning to stir. He is sensible of the meanness of his conduct; he knows that men look on him with disfavour, perhaps with contempt; a recognition of the high and reverend quality of righteousness, and of his obligation as the servant and minister of justice, oppresses him. He awakes to an acknowledgement of his duty. We may suppose that he throws back the bribe in the face of his tempter, and proceeds to give even-handed equity to the clamorous woman.

It is at this point—a very narrow point it is—that the thought of God finds place in this story. "The righteous Lord loveth righteousness." Justice and judgment are the foundation of Jehovah's throne. The Judge of all the earth will do right (Gen. 18:25).

The widow in the parable represents the Church. Her children are defrauded of their inheritance, and she is in an agony on their account. She will dare anything for their sakes. Her resolution is indomitable, because it is sustained by love. She is willing to become a public spectacle, to enter into the most painful situations, to risk bodily peril for herself, if only she may retrieve the calamity of her children. And when she acts thus, God, rising from His throne, gives decree in her favour. The parable seems to speak of vengeance; what it does refer to is legal rectification—a cessation of the injury and a restoration of the right; shall not God do right to His own elect, which cry day and night unto Him, though He bear long with them? I tell you that He will justify them speedily.

He bears long; He suffers long. "God is patient," says St. Augustine, "patient, because He is eternal." But our hopes and fears are narrowed to this little space of time, and we implore Him to make haste. "Though the promise tarry, wait for it; it will not always tarry" (Hab. 2:3). In some good hour—and that hour will be the divinely appointed season—the divine fiat shall go forth; God will interpose. We cannot fathom His reason for delay. They are good and necessary reasons; of this we may be sure. But possible delay in our receiving the answer to our prayers is always to be reckoned with. Therefore our Lord spoke this parable, "to this end, that men ought always to pray and not to faint."

Delay is not denial. The assurance of an answer to believing prayer is based on the character of God. He is "a God of truth and without iniquity, just and right is He" (Deut. 32:4). In prayer we may appeal to the divine righteousness. That, for example, is the force of the warrant which we bring when we pray in the Name of Jesus. In Christ the promises of God, how many soever they be, are all "Yea" (2 Cor. 1:20). Every promise is ours in Christ by an indefeasible right. We may plead each one with an authority like to that with which our glorified Saviour is vested. "Fear not; only believe" (Mark 5:36).

This parable represents a mother praying for her children's welfare. Does it not cover the case of a Christian mother asking God to save her boys and girls? Is it not the fact that most of us who have come to Christ have found the way of life in answer to our mother's prayers? A young man, during the Welsh Revival, was agonizing in a corner of a village chapel. After a time, deliverance came to him. He lifted up a tear-stained face, and shouted, "Well done, Mother!" In another village, a woman, enfeebled and not able to attend the meetings, sat nightly at the door of her cottage as the congregation streamed up the village street. She was waiting to hear news of the homecoming of her boy. Night after night she asked, "Has he come in?" Night after night the answer was, "Not yet." But one evening the neighbours crowded up the street to give her the welcome announcement, "He is in!"

One has difficulty in making an absolute claim on God for the salvation of some for whom we have prayed. We must bow before the divine sovereignty. We may cherish a fervent hope that God will hear our prayer; but we cannot insist that He shall. But in the case of a Christian mother it is different. Her children are within the covenant which is ordered in all things and sure. The Christian family is, in some sense, a unit in the sight of God: "The promise is unto you, and to your children, and to all that are afar off, even as many as the Lord our God shall call" (Acts 2:39). The children of believing parents are in a class by themselves: because of their parents' faith they have a special claim upon God.

But the answer may be long of coming. We read, near the close of our Lord's ministry, that His brethren did not believe in Him (John 7:5). No doubt they were men of excellent character, but they had not committed themselves to the Saviour. In their uprightness they may not have been sensible of their need of redemption. Perhaps it was the Cross of Jesus that convinced them of their need. At all events, very soon after the death on Golgotha, we find them among the waiting saints in the Upper Room. But we think of Mary's prayers for them, and we think of our Lord's intercession. Yet the years passed, and they were still unbelieving when He breathed out His soul to God. Then the answer came. Does it not sometimes happen that a godly mother's prayers remain unanswered through long years of hope deferred? She may even pass from earth without any comfort of assurance in this matter. But the covenant holds.

Before our Lord passes from this parable He turns it toward the expected day of His return. "The Spirit and the Bride say, Come" (Rev. 22:17). The Church is looking upward, waiting for the appearance of the Son of Man from heaven; and scoffers are crying, "Where is the promise of His coming?" (2 Pet. 3:4). The Saviour seems to shade His eyes as He looks piercingly down the vistas of time: "When the Son of Man cometh, shall He find faith on the earth?" He does not say that He will not, but He seems to imply that faith will be hard to come by in the days which precede His advent.

3. The Parable of the Pharisee and the Tax Collector

The Lord Jesus spoke another parable with reference to prayer. It has to do not with the intercession of a redeemed soul for those who are still in darkness, but with the supplication of a sinful man for forgiveness and acceptance.

"Two men went up into the temple to pray; the one a Pharisee, and the other a publican" (Luke 18:10).

"The Pharisee stood and prayed thus with himself." This is not prayer; true prayer is the cry of a needy soul, but this man knows no lack—he is spiritually rich, and increased with goods, and has need of nothing. He is possessed of a satisfying righteousness, negative and positive. Negatively, he is not "as this publican"; positively, he pays tithes of all that he has. With this tenuous covering of his guilty soul he is immeasurably content.

But the publican lifts up his heart to God. Bowed down under an appalling load of guilt, he dare not lift up his eyes to heaven, but beats upon his breast, crying, "O God, be propitiated to me, the sinful one." He cannot believe that any other son of Adam has sinned so grievously as he, the chief of sinners, has done. All his request is for pardoning mercy. Atonement for sin has been provided; for that he craves. It is as if he were making the cry of the penitent king his own: "Purge me with hyssop, and I shall be clean: wash me, and I shall be whiter than snow" (Ps. 51:7). Immediately, while he is yet praying, the answer comes: he is forgiven; he goes down to his house justified.

The chief instruction of this parable is, that a sincere prayer for pardon will be met and honoured without delay. One of those who listened to our Lord's discourse has cast this lesson into a doctrinal form: "If we confess our sins, He is faithful and just to forgive us our sins, and to cleanse us from all unrighteousness" (1 John 1:9).

4. THE UPPER ROOM DISCOURSES

Luther, commenting upon the sacramental discourses preserved in St. John's Gospel (John 13-16), writes, "This is certainly the most choice and comfortable sermon that the Lord Christ uttered in this world. . . . Moreover, herein are most forcibly grounded and settled (as nowhere else in the Scriptures) the true distinctive and chief articles of the Christian belief." What is perhaps the main doctrine insisted upon in these chapters is the worth and power of prayer; and especially this teaching regarding it, that all our prayers are to be presented to the Father in the name of Jesus, and that only in that name may we hope to receive an answer in peace. What our Lord most of all wished to convey to His disciples before He left them was His final instruction regarding the life of prayer.

(a) What are we to understand by the expression, "In My Name" (John 14:13, et al)?

(i) The name of the Lord Jesus is His self-manifestation—all that He has effected by word or act in this world of men. By faith we *abide in Christ*—we make our home in the revelation of the Father which our Lord has given. Therefore we are received into union with Christ in His relation to the Father, according to His own word: "I in them, and Thou in Me" (John 17:23). The sphere of life which the children of faith now inhabit is "Christ." We share His wealth, we are vested in His glory, we are joint-heirs with Him; all that the Father hath is ours in Him. It is in Him therefore that our prayers receive a meet answer.

(ii) To us, living and abiding in Christ, all authority in heaven and on earth is communicated. When we draw near to God the Father, we present our supplications and intercessions in the name of the Only-begotten Son. The prayer-life in Christ acknowledges no frontier, it reaches out to a limitless dominion: "*Whatsoever* ye ask," "If ye shall ask *anything*" (John 14:13-14). There is but one invincible condition: we must ask in the name of Jesus, in harmony with His Spirit, in obedience to His will, in fellowship with Himself. Thus we become partakers with God in the regeneration of the world. Our prayers, inspired by the Holy Ghost, repeat the intercession of the Son of Man, once on earth, and now before the Throne. When the Divine Spirit intercedes within us, "according to God" (Rom. 8:27) it is *in Christ* that we pray.

(iii) But as a man will not lend his name to any enterprise which does not approve itself to his mind, so our Lord Jesus Christ grants His name only to those causes with which He Himself is identified. Therefore He says, "If ye abide in Me, and My words abide in you, ye shall ask what ye will, and it shall be done unto you" (John 15:7). The sayings of Jesus confirm the renewed will, inflaming us with a holy energy to work the works of God. His words challenge us; they are the promises and the entreaties, the warnings and the rebukes, the precepts and exhortations of Him whom we love to term "Lord." As we give heed to these, the word of Christ dwells richly in us. And the words of Christ, as the efflorescence of His very life, are Himself.

To pray in the name of Jesus, therefore, is to pray in Christ.

(b) In describing the prayer-life which is in Christ, our Lord marks out three ways by which the suppliant may come to God. Each of them, however, bears this clear blazon: "In My Name."

(i) Our Lord begins by telling us, for our greater encouragement, that He Himself holds authority to hear and answer prayer: "Whatsoever ye shall ask in My name, that will I do, that the Father may be glorified in the Son. If ye shall ask Me anything in My name, I will do it" (John 14:13-14).

"By these words," says Luther, "He gives us plainly to understand that He is the true Almighty God, equally with the Father." This is undoubtedly implied—He who receives and answers prayer must Himself be very God; but our Lord seems here rather to indicate His place on the Mediatorial Throne, His kingship in the realm of grace. He is about to pass into the Unseen; the land of far distances stretches cold and unwelcoming before the mind of the disciples; but, saith He, "I shall be there, and when you come to the Father in My name, you come to Me." Our Brother is on the Throne, the Nearest of Kin will meet us on the threshold—we see God in the face of Jesus Christ.

(ii) Again, we come by Jesus to the Father: "I chose you . . . that whatsoever ye shall ask of the Father in My name, He may give it to you" (John 15:16). It is not now the Son, but the Father, who receives the petition and grants the request. Sinners as we are, conscious of defilement, confessing our trespasses, we come by the new and living way which our High Priest has inaugurated for us in His flesh, with the name of Jesus on our lips and His blood sprinkled upon our hearts. We are accepted in the name of the Beloved. We stand in Christ; He is made of God unto us righteousness, sanctification, and redemption (1 Cor. 1:30). It is as if our Saviour took our prayers, presenting them to the Father as His own, making request in us, for us. Those prayers which we offer in the name of Jesus He has already presented on His own behalf. He has asked the Father that He may receive the nations for His inheritance and the uttermost parts of the earth for His possession (Ps. 2:8); and He is able to communicate to His people the fruit of His intercession.

(iii) Our union with the Father through Christ is so intimate that our Lord, contemplating our direct entrance into the Holiest, authorizes us to witness to His name before the Father: "If ye shall ask anything of the Father, He will give it you in My name" (John 16:23). It is as if the Father retained the name of Jesus, and we were permitted to go unaccompanied into the Sacred Presence, crying, "Abba, Father." Jesus encourages His followers to enter on this hazard of faith by giving them the most animating assurance of their welcome: "I say not unto you that I will pray the Father for you, for the Father Himself loveth you" (John 16: 26-27). Undoubtedly the Saviour will intercede for His people; He is unchangeably their Advocate before the Throne; the sweetest comfort vouchsafed to us in all our earthly journeyings is that He ever liveth to make intercession for us (Heb. 7:25). But in this crisis of His disciples' faith He is, for the moment, more anxious that they should concentrate attention on another privilege belonging to their divine inheritance: "The Father Himself loveth you, because ye have loved Me, and have believed that I came forth from the Father" (John 16:27). *We do not come in our own right, but we are loved for our own sake.* The Father is not unrighteous to forget our work of faith and labour of love and patience and hope (1 Thess. 1:3; Heb. 6:10), and He loves us because we have been true to His Son, have companied with Him in all His temptations (Luke 22:28), and have borne His name unsullied through a mocking world. We come to the Father, in the name of Jesus, because the Father Himself loveth us.

(c) Our Lord reveals to us in these chapters a three-fold efficacy of prayer in the name of Jesus.

We may name these fields of intercessional activity: service for the kingdom, advancement in personal holiness, a more intimate knowledge of God.

(i) "Verily, verily, I say unto you, He that believeth on Me, the works that I do shall he do also; and greater works than these shall he do; because I go unto the Father. And whatsoever ye shall ask in My name, that will I do" (John 14:12-13). Our Lord is about to ascend from earth to the Right Hand of power, but His mighty works do not cease; they continue in still more glorious manifestations, though now they are accomplished through His Church. It does not appear as if our Lord, in speaking of *greater works,* were contrasting the rapid diffusion of the Gospel after His resurrection with the meagre results of His own ministry; He is rather comparing material wonders with the miracles of grace. At His word the lame walked, the dumb spake, the lepers were cleansed, the eyes of the blind were opened; but under the preaching of the victorious cross and the broken grave, souls that were dead in sins are born into eternal life. No nature-miracle can for one moment be compared with the marvel of sins forgiven and lives renewed. And it is by prayer in the name of Jesus that these things are wrought.

(ii) "Ye did not choose Me, but I chose you, and appointed you, that ye should go and bear fruit, and that your fruit should abide; that whatsoever ye shall ask of the Father in My name, He may give it you" (John 15:16).

Fruit is for nourishment and delectation, therefore St. Paul writes to the Church in Rome: "That I might have some fruit in you also, even as in the rest of the Gentiles" (Rom. 1:13). In this sense the word is employed in the epitaph of Count von Zinzendorf, the founder of the *Unitas Fratrum*: "He was ordained that he should bring forth fruit, and fruit that should remain." But in the fifteenth chapter of John our Lord seems to use this word in a different sense. The fruit of the vine is the expression of its life, and this life robes itself in all those virtues which made the Son of Man so radiantly fair in the eyes of those who see wisdom. "The fruit of the Spirit is love, joy, peace, long- suffering, kindness, goodness, faithfulness, meekness, self-control" (Gal. 5:22-23). Not one star in all this galaxy must be allowed to grow dim; all must shine with increasing lustre, until holiness be perfected in the fear of the Lord. And holiness is won by earnest and continuous prayer in the holy name of Jesus.

(iii) "In that day ye shall ask Me nothing. Verily, verily, I say unto you, If ye shall ask anything of the Father, He will give it you in My name. Hitherto have ye asked nothing in My name: ask, and ye shall receive, that your joy may be fulfilled. These things have I spoken unto you in parables: the hour cometh, when I shall no more speak unto you in parables, but shall tell you plainly of the Father" (16:23-25).

It is as if He said, "I am going away. You will not henceforth be able to come to Me in bodily presence, questioning Me about many things—I go to the Father. But it is better so; it is expedient for you that I go away. Henceforth I will speak to you not in figures and comparisons drawn from material things, but in spiritual language. This teaching will pass through your own mind, and become a personal possession; it will bring to your knowledge heavenly things in a speech more apprehensive, more sure, than that of earth." Eye hath not seen, nor ear heard, neither have entered into the heart of man, the things which God hath prepared for those who love Him—but they are being revealed by the Holy Spirit (1 Cor. 2:9-20). St. John, remembering these sayings of Christ, delivered them anew to his little children in Ephesus: "Ye have an anointing from the Holy One, and ye know all things. . . . And as for you, the anointing which ye received of Him abideth in you, and ye need not that any one teach you; but as His anointing teacheth you concerning all things, and is true, and is no lie, and even as it taught you, ye abide in Him" (1 John 2:20, 27).

The loftiest privilege of the Christian faith is that we should enter into the excellency of the knowledge of Christ, daily becoming acquainted with Him in clearer recognition and ampler experience, learning daily and hourly the fullness of His grace and the riches of His glory, until, in the contemplation of His measureless mercy, we are "lost in wonder, love, and praise." And it is by prayer in the name of Jesus that we attain to this most excellent knowledge.

All this, in the absence of Christ, and while He tarries. The name of Christ, which signifies His self-revelation, reminds us also that He has withdrawn Himself from earth for a time. It is precisely this absence which introduces us to those vast fields of intercession which invite us to new acts of communion with our Lord. When He returns in the glory of the Kingdom, apart from sin, unto salvation, prayer will give place to praise and adoration. Until then, all our petitions express themselves as a sigh for His appearing. "The Spirit and the Bride say, Come" (Rev. 22:17). "Come, Lord Jesus, come quickly."

"Ask, and ye shall receive," said our Saviour, "that your joy may be fulfilled" (John 16:24). The depth of our prayerfulness is the measure of our gladness.

CHAPTER 10

The High-Priestly Prayer

"Put off thy shoes from off thy feet, for the place whereon thou standest is holy ground" (Exod. 3:5). No spot on earth is nearer heaven than the shaded recess in the valley of the Kidron, where our Lord and His disciples arrested their steps for a time on the way to Gethsemane. Melanchthon says, "Nothing more dignified, nothing more holy, nothing more fruitful, nothing more pathetic has ever been heard in heaven or earth, than this prayer of the very Son of God." And another adds this testimony: "This prayer is solitary among all the prayers of mankind, separated from all others by a perfect illumination, which is at the same time a perfect repose. It has no voice of confession, deprecation, supplication; no echo, however distant, of recognition of sin, no tone that is touched with a feeling of demerit or defect; only the certain consciousness, 'I have glorified Thee on the earth; I have finished the work which Thou gavest Me to do.' There is no intimation of infirmity or entreaty for help; for self only one request, 'Glorify Thy Son, that Thy Son also may glorify Thee.'" This witness is true. No words ever uttered in the audience of men are more divine than those of our Saviour's intercessory prayer. In this illustrious chapter—"the sanctuary of the universe," it has been called—we see the glory of God streaming through the veil of flesh.

The late Dean Vaughan confessed that it was only with "a painful effort" that he could nerve himself to read this prayer of intercession in public. The greatest expositors have scarcely dared to make its profound sentences the theme of their discourse. Our Lord's Prayer of Consecration is indeed the sacredest shrine of Scripture, the Holiest of all. Yet it has been given for our instruction, and we may not turn from the consideration of it, even at the bidding of reverence. For it is doctrine as well as prayer. It is addressed to the minds of the disciples as directly as to the ear of God. All the varied discourse at the Supper Table is gathered together and certified in this priestly utterance. "This prayer of Christ," writes Calvin, "was a sealing of the precious teaching, as well that it should be ratified in itself, as that it should create firm faith in His disciples." And many a soul has found comfort in a dark hour through these words. When John Knox, the Scottish Reformer, came to the brink of the silent river, he said to his wife, "Go, read where I cast my first anchor." She read the seventeenth chapter of St. John's Gospel, after which he fell asleep. Spener the Pietist also, though he had never ventured to preach upon this chapter, greatly loved it; as his end drew near, he asked those who surrounded his couch to read it aloud to him. When they had done so, he said, "Again"; after that, at his renewed request, they read it a third time. Then he confessed that it seemed to him that the true understanding of this prayer transcends the measure of faith which the Lord is wont to impart to His disciples during their pilgrimage. Here there are deeps beyond deeps and heights surmounting heights. We are constrained to say of these words what Job confessed with regard to the mysteries of nature: "Lo, these are but the outskirts of His ways, and how small a whisper do we hear of Him, but the thunder of His mighty deeds who can understand?" (Job 26:14).

This chapter falls into three sections, each distinguished by a special use of the Sacred Name—"Father," "Holy Father," "Righteous Father." Our Lord, speaking for Himself, uses the simple word "Father" as no other can, for He is Son by absolute right. Afterward, when He makes intercession for His disciples, He addresses the Deity as "Holy Father," for He is the Author of holiness in those who believe. And at the close of the prayer, He speaks of God as "Righteous Father" for it is in righteousness that He has revealed Himself to the world of men.

1. "Father"

"These things spake Jesus, and lifting up His eyes to heaven, He said, 'Father, the hour is come; glorify Thy Son, that the Son may glorify Thee.'" The Father is as near to Jesus as the disciples are; His presence is as manifest. Our High Priest presents Himself to the Father, reporting the fulfilment of the task assigned to Him, acknowledging as "His own" those whom the Father had given Him.

The Father had given to the Son, in the ages before time, a people of redemption. These He covenanted to call, redeem, and sanctify, in the shedding of His own blood: they were predestinated as His inheritance, His glory and joy.

With these there was granted to the Son power over all flesh, that He should give eternal life to those whom He had received. The fullness of the Spirit's grace, resting on the Son and ministered through Him, was to be the divine agency effecting the new birth in those who should believe.

This new birth was to be the entrance of the redeemed on eternal life—a life like God's own—a life of holiness and truth, of growing conformity to the likeness of Christ. For "this is life eternal, to know Thee the only true God and Him whom Thou didst send, even Jesus Christ" (John 17:3).

Our Saviour claims the promised bestowment in the right of His obedience unto death. He does not supplicate, He requires (vs. 9, 15, 20); He does not implore, He wills (v. 24). He anticipates His death, presenting His prayer with authority because of it: "Father, the hour is come" (John 17:1). That hour which has been drawing near through unnumbered ages of measureless grace, is an hour of sorrow and dismay, of victory and rejoicing, an hour central in the history of the world and in the life of God. Already, in the Master's view, that hour has approached and gone. His life is rendered up with acceptance: "I glorified Thee on the earth, having accomplished the work which Thou hast given Me to do" (John 17:4). He lifts up an unblemished sacrifice to God, and claims the promised reward.

The contrast between this prayer and that of Gethsemane, offered on the same evening and with only a brief space of time between, is startling. *Here* the outshining of the divine glory is so overpowering that the sharpness of death, the ignominy of the Cross, and even the agony of forsakenness are unheeded—it is as if they were already past. *There* the unutterable anguish of the Sin-bearer seems to blot out of the heavens the light of the Father's face. In either case we are dealing with magnitudes that are greater than any measuring rod can mete—infinite love, unutterable pain. The difference seems to lie in this: in the one case our Saviour is gazing with undimmed eyes on the unveiled Presence, and His human heart rises in rapture, saying, "Now come I to Thee"; in the other, He has humbled Himself to receive a pre-libation of the bitter cup. "Let this cup pass from Me. The cup which the Father hath given Me, shall I not drink it?" (Matt. 26:39; John 18:11).

As our Lord presents His finished work to the Father, He makes this one request: "And now, O Father, glorify Thou Me with Thine own self with the glory which I had with Thee before the world was" (v. 5). The hour has come for the recall of the Ambassador from a distant country, the return of the Son to His ancestral home. The mission of the Eternal Word began "before the world was"—His goings forth were from ancient days, from everlasting. In the divine prevision our Lord was foreordained to be a sacrifice before the foundation of the world (1 Pet. 1:20); in the gift of the Father's love the Lamb of God was slain ere time had begun its course (Rev. 13:8). Throughout all ages this high eternal covenant pointed forward to the fullness of the times when the Word became incarnate and the Son clothed Himself in our nature. Bishop Westcott says concisely, "Whatever men have found to kindle hope lies all in the few syllables, 'the Word became flesh'; and I cannot conceive anything which can go beyond it." In becoming man, our Lord humbled Himself, became poor, laid aside the dignities and glories of His high estate, and came forth from God. Now, He is about to resume the divine mode of being, dwelling in the sweet immediacy of holy love with the Father, face to face in co-equal union. In an attempt to explain the unexplainable, the doctors of the Latin

Church were accustomed to say that the Son went forth from the Bosom of God, without leaving it. While on earth, He was still in heaven (John 3:13; 12:26; 14:3; 17:24). But in His coming, there was privation, and the feeling of absence. Now He prays for a return to the full, unclouded fellowship of the eternal years: "Glorify Thou Me with Thine own self." The sentence is pregnant: it implies the *presence* and the *possession* of God, without limit or restraint. The Son of Man returns to His eternal home.

In the 22nd verse the Saviour says, "The glory which Thou hast given Me I have given unto them." In Christ we also are introduced into the Presence of God and are privileged to become possessors of His fullness. We are joint-heirs with Christ, and "there is nothing alien in God"; "God, even our own God, shall bless us" (Ps. 67:6).

Here are some of the gifts which our Lord had during the years of His ministry bestowed upon "His own" and which we also may receive out of His fullness, grace upon grace.

(a) "I have manifested Thy name unto the men whom Thou gavest Me out of the world" (v. 6). The Lord Jesus is the revelation of the Father. He is the effulgence of His glory and the express image of His person (Heb. 1:3). The divine glory shone through our Lord's human vesture more and more clearly as His passion grew still more intense, until, on that night in which He was betrayed, He was able to say, "He that hath seen Me hath seen the Father" (John 14:9).

(b) "The words which Thou gavest Me I have given unto them" (v. 8). This reference includes both the sayings and doings of the Lord Jesus, which, taken together, constitute the revelation of the Son in His unspotted holiness and unutterable love. To receive His "words" is to receive Himself.

(c) "While I was with them, I kept them in Thy name, which Thou hast given Me; and I guarded them, and not one of them perished, but the son of perdition, that the Scripture might be fulfilled" (v. 12). The shadow of sin falls across the glory that fills that Upper Room. Until the end of all things, when God shall present the complete vindication of the moral government of the world, sin shall remain an insoluble mystery—sin in its permission and continuance.

All but the son of loss have been preserved from loss; they have been shielded under the prayers, the warnings, and the high example of their blessed Lord; walking in His footsteps they have not erred; through faith they have been guarded "unto a salvation ready to be revealed in the last time" (1 Pet. 1:5).

2. "HOLY FATHER"

In the second division of this prayer the Saviour commends to the Father those who by gift and purchase are "His own" (John 13:1). Six times at least in this short chapter the Lord Jesus repeats the words, "Those whom Thou hast given Me." Believers are inexpressibly dear to Him as being the Father's gift; they are precious also because they are the subjects of His redeeming love. For them His petition is, that they may become holy. The sanctification which He implores on their behalf comes from the Name and Being of God, and consists principally in three articles: that they may be kept from the evil that is in the world (v. 11); that they may be perfected together in love (v. 21); and that they may have their dwelling with Him in regions unseen and eternal (v. 24).

"Holy Father . . . make them holy." These words are central to the second part of the Prayer of Intercession. They were uttered in confirmation of our Lord's petition that His people might be hallowed: "For their sakes I sanctify Myself, that they also may be sanctified in truth" (v. 19).

(a) "Holy Father . . . make them holy." Holiness has its ground in God. It is only in the measure in which we are assimilated to the Divine Nature that we are sanctified.

The holiness is inscrutable; it is of dazzling splendour; He dwells in light that is inaccessible and full of glory (1 Tim. 6:16). We discern it only as we resign ourselves to its sacred influences; we are changed into its semblance only as we draw near.

(i) In our creation we are framed within the likeness of Deity. Our true bent is toward Him who alone is holy. The consent of our manifold impulses aspires toward that harmony which characterizes the divine perfection. Upon each distinguishing virtue is imprinted the imperative of the rule of God: "Be ye therefore perfect, even as our Father which is in heaven is perfect" (Matt. 5:48).

(ii) The natural craving for symmetry of character which belongs to us as our birthright is reinforced by the grace of the Holy Spirit who works in us to will and to do according to the Father's good pleasure. We advance as in a journey, we strive as in a contest, we toil toward an end; at last we come to the fullness of the perfect life.

> One step more, and the goal receives us;
>> One word more, and life's task is done;
> One toil more, and the cross is carried—
>> And sets the sun.

(iii) The measure of this perfection is the full stature of the Christ. In the beauty of His character our Lord has met the aspirations of the soul athirst for God, and has transcended them. All our loftiest ideals are fulfilled; yet this is only the beginning of the soul's itinerary toward God. The rule of the road is, "He that saith he abideth in Him ought himself also so to walk even as He walked" (1 John 2:6). And at every step we recognize some new trait of goodness in our adorable Master. Day by day, in our enlarging experience, He is, as it were, transfigured before us. The most glorious achievements of the saints are but the glancing radiance that falls from the white splendour of His renown. He towers above our attainments as the stars lift themselves above the hills, but our hopes soar upwards through vast regions of the spirit, defying extinction; for "we know that if He shall be manifested, we shall be like Him, for we shall see Him as He is" (1 John 3:2).

(b) Such is the holiness of Christ. What was the method of His sanctification? Only here does He speak explicitly of it. "For their sakes," He says, "I sanctify Myself."

The root meaning of the word "sanctify" is *consecrate*. One who is dedicated to God becomes, by the very necessity of His self-oblation to the thrice-holy One, himself holy.

Between the consecration of the Son of God and our own an important distinction is marked. "Sanctify Thou them," He prays—we are sanctified through Him. But He is the priest of His own consecration: "I sanctify Myself." For He is not as we are. We are sinners; He is sinless. We are saved by grace; He is the Saviour. We are ignorant and erring; He is a High Priest chosen from among men in things pertaining to God. We are being sanctified through the Word; He is Himself the Word which sanctifies.

And yet, in perfect harmony with this contrast, there is a parallelism between His self-consecration and ours. We have seen that holiness in us involves our being kept in the will of God, our being fulfilled in love, our being raised into the new life of the Spirit. In all these respects the Son of the Blessed, who is also Man of our manhood, affirms, "I sanctify Myself."

(i) *The Lord Jesus held Himself resolutely and unshakenly within the will of His Father.* In the beginning, as He has told us, the Father consecrated Him and sent Him into the world. His response was, "Lo, I am come; in the volume of the book it is prescribed to Me: I delight to do Thy will, O My God; yea, Thy law is within My heart" (Psalm 40:7-8). Commenting on these words, a New Testament writer presents this interpretation: "By the which will we are sanctified through the offering of the body of Jesus Christ once for all" (Heb. 10:10).

In His humiliation our Lord became obedient to law. He proceeded to honour the will of His Father, to fulfil the commission entrusted to Him. From the beginning He foreknew that His way to the Throne lay through sacrifice. In spite of the natural shrinking of our human flesh from pain, in defiance of the solicitations of the evil one, He set His face, and went unswervingly down the appointed way of the holy Cross. Now He stands at the crisis of His life of self-sacrifice. He came to our earth, that He might minister to the needy, and ministering give His life (Mark 10:45). So that actually He took our manhood, that He might lay it down. He became incarnate, that He might die. At last, the hour to which He has long been hastening has struck. Swiftly the Father will withdraw from His beloved Son the light of His Presence, the comfort of His strengthening arm. Our Lord stands almost at the gate of the Olive Garden, where the anguish is to fall on Him to the uttermost. The divine indignation against sin is about to be poured into a cup of trembling which He shall receive from the hand of the Father. Yet with calmness He confronts the hour of desolation as it is about to strike, and advances to greet the holy, acceptable, and perfect will of God. "For their sakes, I sanctify Myself."

This joyful obedience was an essential element in the great reconciliation. "It was not His suffering so much as His willingness to suffer that pleased the Father," says Bernard of Clairvaux. In the same strain, Calvin avers, "The obedience of Christ is the most important circumstance of His death." Almost to the same effect our Lord has said, "Therefore doth My Father love Me, because I lay down My life, that I may take it again" (John 10:17).

(ii) *In this we see the final gift of love.* It was in love that our Saviour came into the world: "Ye know the grace of our Lord Jesus Christ that, though He was rich, yet for your sakes He became poor, that ye through His poverty might become rich" (2 Cor. 8:9). All the path of His progress was strewn with the largesse that betokened His triumph. He gave royally, extravagantly, without measure or calculation—He gave all that Godhead could bestow. Now one thing only remains to Him unyielded—His life. And this He is about to offer, as the completion of the divine gift of Himself. To the last reserve of His being He yields Himself to those who are His friends; so that they may say, as if they stood alone in the world, "He loved me, and gave Himself for me."

He gave Himself generously, lovingly, joyfully. He embraced the Cross; the day on which He confronted death amid its darkest terrors was the day of the gladness of His heart. His divine charity in resistless flood overleapt the last barrier that would impede its progress, and poured itself out over the world in torrents of sovereign compassion. It is evident that even as our Lord was uttering this calm Prayer of Intercession the storm-filled petitions of the 22nd Psalm was pulsing through His mind in a strong undercurrent of thought and feeling (see Psalm 22:22 with John 17:6, 26). Yet how completely is the storm brought to a hushed serenity within the divine quietude. The psalm of the breaking heart has become a song in the night, as when a holy solemnity is kept, and gladness of heart as when one goeth with a melody to come into the mountain of the Lord, to the Rock of Israel.

In the Palace of Versailles there is a magnificent gallery dedicated "to all the glories of France." There is a long succession of battle-pieces, each one commemorating a triumph. The victorious generals are represented, for the most part, in some safe position on the field, in immaculate clothing, with untarnished lace and unruffled plumes. Far off one sees the baleful light of flaming towns; at a considerable distance the blast of artillery is depicted and the clash of opposing squadrons. To all this conventional art there is one exception. A great fight has been won, but at a fearful price; and now the victors are bringing home to its last resting-place the body of the dead leader. The lifeless form is supported on horseback by two dragoons, the white face is turned to the sky, and behind, the soldiers, with drooping heads, march in pained silence. Victory has been achieved, but the leader's life is forfeit.

It was only by uttermost self-sacrifice that the world was redeemed, only by uttermost self- sacrifice shall it be saved. "For their sakes," as He opens His hands to receive the rending nails; "for their sakes," as He bares His soul to the pitiless tempest, when all God's waves and billows pass over Him; "for their sakes, I sanctify Myself."

(iii) But the death of the Leader of God's embattled host, although the forfeit of the war, was not the end. It is Christ that died; yea, rather, that is risen again, and is become the firstfruits of earth's full harvest. Accordingly, we find that *our Lord here is consecrating Himself for entrance on His heavenly ministry.*

Jesus of Nazareth, girt with the simple purity of His nature and apparelled in the beautiful garments of His perfected obedience, stands on the threshold of His heavenly ministry. The path which led to that high office had stooped to the portals of the grave. Already, in this final consecration of His Person and Work, He has saluted and virtually endured the Cross. In surrendering Himself to death He has, as it were, already died. He has forded the brook by the way, and now has His dwelling in the eternal light. Listen to His own words: "Father, I have finished the work which Thou gavest Me to do. . . .Now I am no more in the world. . . .I come to Thee. . . .That which Thou hast given Me, I will that, where I am, they also may be with Me." Thus our Lord's consecration bears Him into heaven. He had been pressing forward to this priestly ministry, not only during His earthly years, but also from of old, even from everlasting.

He had set His face toward Jerusalem that, having died, He might rise again, and so communicate to men His own deathless life. The resurrection of Christ is the true term of His life in the flesh. For it was in His rising from the dead, and in His clothing Himself with a spiritual body, that the human Sonship of the Eternal Word was fulfilled, according to the inspired sentence: "Thou art My Son; this day have I begotten Thee" (Acts 13:33). And in this perfection of holy Manhood He is the figure of the ransomed Church, the First-born among many brethren:

> For me, Lord Jesus, Thou hast died,
>> And I have died in Thee.
> Thou'rt risen; my bands are all untied,
>> And now Thou liv'st in me.
> When purified, made white, and tried,
>> Thy glory then for me.

This new life into which the Redeemer leads His people is a life where reconciliation is perfected and victory is secured. It is a life lived in heavenly places, enriched by the bestowment of the Holy Spirit, and powerfully wrought upon by the intercession of Jesus Christ.

(c) In those particulars in which our Lord consecrated Himself to His high office of mediation the believer discovers the method of his own sanctification.

It is in the virtue of Christ's overcoming that He intercedes for us: "Holy Father, keep them in Thy name which Thou hast given Me. . . . keep them from the evil" (vs. 11, 15). This prayer, offered as of right by our glorified Redeemer, surrounds us as with a wall of defence. Into this sanctuary the enemy and the avenger cannot come. Dwelling within it, we are free from the noise of alarms, from the fear of failure and falling: "He will not suffer thy foot to be moved; He that keepeth Thee will not slumber. Behold, He that keepeth Israel shall neither slumber nor sleep. . . . The Lord shall keep Thee from all evil; He shall keep thy soul. The Lord shall keep thy going out and thy coming in, from this time forth, and for evermore" (Psalm 121).

(i) *It is a prayer for daily shelter within the will of God.* "Holy Father, keep them. . . . keep them from the evil."

Life is dangerous in the extreme; its ways are perilous. An unguarded moment may bring a lifetime's regret, an unchecked desire may precipitate a shattering fall. The possibility of lasting failure lurks within us in our unsanctified impulses, surrounds us on every hand in the concourse of assailing temptations, and confronts us terribly in the direct assault of a personal evil spirit. But God is able to keep us from falling, and to present us faultless before the presence of His glory with exceeding joy (Jude 24). He is able to uphold in the safe ways of His direction even our weak, wayward feet.

There is a touching expression at the close of St. John's First Epistle. All through the argument of that great doctrinal treatise the aged apostle has been summoning his little children to a strenuous war within. Life is a conflict, keen even to agony. Every mental power must be engaged, force must be intensified to the last degree, all the faculties, knit in stern accord, must be strained to the last point of effort. But at the close the trustful soul, in the full surrender of faith, flings itself in entire repose into the arms of Christ: "He that was begotten of God keepeth him" (1 John 5:18).

(ii) *It is a prayer that love may be made perfect.* Love to Christ first, then to His people, and finally to those who are ready to perish, but for whom the Saviour died. Love made perfect is holiness in the highest degree. "I in them, and Thou in Me, that they may be made perfect in one; and that the world may know that Thou didst send Me, and lovedst them, even as Thou hast loved Me" (John 17:23).

The love of God was perfected toward us in the Cross of our Lord Jesus Christ; and as in faith and obedience we dwell there, that love is perfected in us. We stand in wonder and praise in the presence of this great mystery, the pained love of God; we open our hearts to receive it, we welcome its gracious influences, our cold hearts are kindled in its sacred flame—we "love His love." Dr. Griffith Thomas, in a recent volume, quotes a sentence from Dr. Whipple, Bishop of Minnesota, to the effect that for thirty years he had endeavoured to see the face of Christ in the countenances of those with whom he disagreed. That is the true spirit of love, to cherish the unthankful and the evil, to esteem others better than ourselves, to rejoice in the discovery of God's favour toward those with whom we differ.

(iii) *Lastly, this is a prayer for fellowship with Christ in heavenly places.* "Father, I will that they also whom Thou hast given Me be with Me where I am." This petition will be answered in it fullness in the heavenly state; it is being answered daily in the gift of a heavenly experience. Life is a continuous following in the footsteps of the Risen Lord. We dwell with Him in His resurrection; we are shielded and strengthened by His most potent intercession; we are partakers with Him in the promise of the Father, and are with Him enriched by spiritual gifts; we wait in fellowship with Him for the glad hour of His return. Christ and His people are united in such firm bonds that they shall never be sundered. Blaise Pascal prayed in an hour of great spiritual exaltation: "Jesus Christ! Jesus Christ! Jesus Christ! I have renounced Him, I have fled from Him, I have separated myself from Him; may I never be separated from Him again!"

Now this, says our Lord, is being sanctified *in truth.* Not "by the truth" as the instrument of our sanctification—that is spoken of in verse 17—but here, in verse 19, the Saviour asks for our thorough, perfected, and complete sanctification. Let St. Paul interpret for us those awe-inspiring words: "The God of peace Himself sanctify you wholly; and may your spirit and soul and body be preserved entire, without blame, at the presence of our Lord Jesus Christ. Faithful is He that calleth you, who also will do it" (1 Thess. 5:23-24).

Now to our God whose power can do
More than our wants or wishes know,
Be everlasting honour done
In all the Church, through Christ, the Son.

In Rubens' famous cartoon, "The Triumph of Religion," the chariot of the truth is borne onward resistlessly. All forces that make for unhappiness or which tend to evil are led in captivity behind it: hunger, and sickness, and war, and the evil one himself, follow in chains. But on the car there are only two figures—Faith and Love. Faith has flung her arms round the gaunt, unshapely cross of unhewn wood, whereas Love is standing erect, lifting on high a radiant cup of blessing. This, in the view of the painter, is pure religion and undefiled—Faith embracing the cross, and Love bestowing benediction. Had I been a painter, I think I should have added a third figure, that of Hope, with the day-star upon her brow, looking upwards for His appearing, and whispering, her lips tremulous with emotion, "It is not yet made manifest what we shall be. We know that, if He shall be manifested, we shall be like Him, for we shall see Him as He is" (1 John 3:2).

Archbishop Leighton, giving charge to the clergy of his diocese, conjuring them to perfect their holiness in the fear of the Lord, anticipated a reflection which might arise in the minds of some of those whom he addressed. This is what he wrote: "But you will possibly say, 'What does he himself that speaks these things to us?' Alas, I am ashamed to tell you. All I dare say is this: I think I see the beauty of holiness, and am enamoured of it, though I attain it not; and howsoever little I attain, would rather live and die in the pursuit of it, than in the pursuit, yea, in the possession and enjoyment, though unpurified, of all the advantages that this world affords. And I trust, dear brethren, you are of the same opinion, and have the same desire and design, and follow it both more diligently and with better success."

3. "RIGHTEOUS FATHER"

It is in righteousness that God makes Himself known as Father to the world of men. It is as Christ's Father that He allows us to call Him by that endearing name, and Christ is the Righteous One. This expression, which recurs so often in the New Testament, is borrowed from the passion-song of the Servant of Jehovah (Isa. 53:11).

Righteous in all His ways as the Suffering Messiah is, it is particularly because He has come under the Father's mandate to magnify the law and make it honourable, to restore that which He had not taken away, and to become sin for us though He knew no sin, that He is styled by the Evangelical Prophet "Jehovah's Righteous Servant." It is as the Sin-bearer, the stainless Sufferer, the atoning Lamb, that He is revealed to a world of sinners guilty and condemned. There is one Lawgiver who is able to save, One who has met the challenge and satisfied the claims of the avenging law, who is Himself "just and the Justifier" of the ungodly. He—He Himself, in His doing and His dying—is the propitiation for our sins, and not for ours only, but also for the whole world (1 John 2:2).

Earlier in this prayer, the Saviour said, "I pray for them: I pray not for the world, but for those whom Thou hast given Me" (v. 9). This particular request He makes for "His own"—that they may be holy. The world cannot be partaker in His intercession at this point; but afterwards He will intercede for them. Two things He will ask—that they may believe (v. 21) and that they many know (v 23). He asks that they may believe in His divine mission, and that they may know the love of God toward them to be as the love which He bears to the Son.

(a) "That the world may believe that Thou didst send Me" (v. 21).

The object of saving faith is variously indicated in the New Testament. Sometimes we are commanded to believe the words which our Saviour has spoken, at other times we are enjoined to believe in His name—His self-manifestation on earth. Again, we are invited to trust in His person; but always this act of saving faith terminates in God. All these modes of belief are signified in this brief sentence: "That the world may believe that Thou didst send Me." We trust Himself, because of the life He lived, the works He accomplished, the words He spoke; and more than all, because He has come bearing a divine commission: "My Father sent Me," He says, "and I am come." Thus the faith that saves is ultimately faith in the Father of our Lord Jesus Christ, and our Father.

(b) "That the world may know that Thou didst send Me, and lovedst them, even as Thou lovedst Me" (v. 23). Faith becomes assurance, trust brightens into knowledge. Vinet asserts that the full assurance of faith is not the belief that we are saved, but that we are loved.

In its initial acting, faith is simply faith; "faith unformed" the Reformers styled it; "naked faith" said the devout churchman of the Middle Ages. "Faith alone saves," protested Melanchthon, "but the faith that saves is not alone." Yet in the act of affiance whereby the soul is united to Christ, it seems to be alone:

> Nothing in my hand I bring,
> Simply to Thy Cross I cling.

A singular reliance on Christ is the primary act of saving faith. This is, as the fathers of the Secession were accustomed to say, "a venturesome believing."

But when faith creates experience, knowledge is the fruit of this act of affiance: "We know whom we have believed" (2 Tim. 1:12). And in the knowledge of Him who is our Saviour we know that He has come as the witness of a love which passes knowledge, and which the strongest faith can only feebly grasp: "That the world may know that Thou didst send Me, and lovedst them, even as Thou lovedst Me." Behold, what manner of love!

> So near, so very near to God;
>   I cannot nearer be;
> For in the person of His Son,
>   I am as near as He.

> So dear, so very dear to God;
>   I cannot dearer be;
> The love wherewith He loves the Son,
> Such is His love to me.

And now, in order that the world in all its history may *believe* and *know,* the Saviour carries the burden of this marvellous prayer right to the bounds of time: "O righteous Father, the world knew Thee not, but I knew Thee, and these knew that Thou didst send Me. And I have made known unto them Thy name, and will make it known; that the love wherewith Thou lovedst Me may be in them, and I in them" (v. 25).

Our Lord came to this earth, not merely to save those who were lost, but to reveal the Father. In the ages before His advent, men had become familiar with the thought of the divine holiness, goodness, and truth. But the power and passion of His love could not be made known until in human nature He had confronted the sin that marred our peace, had assumed our guilt, and died our death. The Father gave His Son to die; the Spirit sealed Him for His atoning sacrifice, and the Son came, laying His life down of Himself. The feelings of Abraham as he stood by the altar of Moriah, unsheathing the knife to slay his only son, Isaac, whom he loved (Gen. 22), present us with what is perhaps the nearest Old Testament figure of the suffering love of God, when He hid His face from the Beloved and was pleased to put Him to grief (Isa. 53:10).

The divine righteousness was known to the fathers. Justice and judgment, they said, are the foundation of the eternal Throne. The ways of the Lord are right; whatever He doeth is according to equity and truth. In His sovereign procedure there is no shadow cast by turning (James 1:17). His kingly titles are "Faithful" and "True," and in righteousness He doth judge and make war (Rev. 19:11). But it is in the dread conflict with sin that the potency of the divine righteousness is fully disclosed. Jehovah had sworn by Himself that at any cost, even in the death of His dear Son, He would break the power of sin. This He has done by judging sin in the death of the Lord Jesus. "Through the knowledge of Himself shall My righteous Servant make many righteous; and He shall bear their iniquities" (Isa. 53:11).

The holiness of God has been made the theme of age-long praise. The prophets sang the trisagion (Isa. 6:3) and the Psalmist re-echoed the strain (Ps. 99:3, 5, 9). The law also commanded the attainment of a purity like to that of God (Lev. 19:2). Now, however, through all the Christian years, in the experience of all saints, the measure of the divine holiness is seen to pass beyond our human reach. It shines infinitely far above us, yet it is the goal to which we aspire. More and more, as we apprehend the surpassing perfection of the Holy One, we are changed into the same likeness, from glory to glory, in the presence and by the Spirit of the Lord.

CHAPTER 11

In the Olive Garden

"Put off thy shoes from off thy feet," said the Lord to Moses, when he turned aside to see the bush that burned and was not consumed; "the place whereon thou standest is holy ground" (Exod. 3:5). One scarcely dares speak of Gethsemane and the midnight conflict, where our Redeemer agonised and overcame. Angels may have gathered round in awful reverence to gaze upon the suppliant Saviour, "who in the days of His flesh, having offered up prayers and supplications with strong crying and tears unto Him that was able to save Him out of death, and having been heard for His godly fear, though He was a Son, yet learned obedience by the things which He suffered" (Heb 5: 7-8); but the very chiefest apostles could not endure to watch with their Lord one hour (Matt. 26:40).

St. Luke tells us that Jesus, having left the Upper Room, "went, as His custom was, unto the Mount of Olives; and the disciples also followed Him" (Luke 22:39). When He came to Jerusalem, to celebrate the great festivals, Gethsemane was, apparently, His resting-place for the night (Luke 21:37). He did not remain in the city, partly because He loved the simplicities of nature; partly, it is possible, because He was a poor man, and could not meet the cost of lodgings within the walls; but chiefly, we may suppose, because He desired privacy for prayer. How often, when the disciples had drawn their mantles round them and were pillowing their heads on the gnarled root of some olive tree, may not our Lord have watched and wept! We can imagine His fixed gaze, as the marble towers of the temple shone in the moon-light, and the heedless city slept, while the day of visitation was shaking out its swiftly running sands. "O Jerusalem, Jerusalem, which killest the prophets, and stonest them that are sent unto her, how often would I have gathered thy children together, even as a hen gathereth her chickens under her wings, and ye would not!" (Luke 13:34). May not ejaculations such as these, mingled with "tears" and enforced with "strong crying," have often interpreted the Saviour's silent communing with His Father?

There is a surprising contrast between the serenity of our Lord's High-Priestly Prayer and the overwhelming distress that shook His soul in Gethsemane's agony. He was sorrowful, exceeding sorrowful, sorrowful even unto death; He was greatly amazed and sore troubled; consternation possessed His spirit. Two things had come to pass: in the Upper Room He had said, "The prince of the world cometh, and he hath nothing in Me" (John 14:30); and in the Valley of the Kidron He had prayed, "Father, the hour is come" (John 17:1). That hour, foreordained through all the eternities, an hour of anguish and dread, had darkened upon the soul of the Messiah, and Satan entered into the darkness, to assail the suffering Saviour with all the malice and craft of hell. The Captain of our salvation chose His battleground with judgment. In this place of prayer, hallowed by numberless seasons of communion with His Father, He will meet the adversary and withstand the shock of His onset. Our Redeemer did not shun the grasp of death: "To die is but to fall asleep, on the kind arms of God." Nor was He greatly afraid of pain; it is His strength that has enabled the martyr saints to tread the lion and the adder underfoot. But soul and spirit recoiled from the doom of sin, due to mankind, and accepted by the Surety. The word which He employs, "this cup" (Luke 22:42), has reference, we believe, to the words with which He instituted the Feast of Remembrance: "This is My blood of the covenant which is shed for many unto remission of sins" (Matt. 26:28). The cup betokens His sacrificial offering for the sins of men. To us it offers heaven's richest benediction; to Him it brought unutterable pain.

> Death and the curse was in our cup;
> O Christ, 'twas full for Thee!
> But Thou hast drained the last drop;
> 'Tis empty now for me:
> That bitter cup,
> Love drank it up;
> Now blessing's draught for me.

According to the First Gospel, which gives us the most consecutive account of our Lord's conflict in the Olive Garden, Jesus offered two distinct prayers—the second one repeated and prolonged. The first is given by St. Matthew in these words: "O My Father, if it be possible, let this cup pass away from Me: nevertheless, not as I will, but as Thou wilt" (Matt. 26:39).

The Saviour asks if there may not be some other way of deliverance for mankind than that which exacts a measureless ransom price. From of old the Father has been devising means whereby His banished should not be expelled from Him. Is this the only way that infinite wisdom can discover? Is salvation impossible to men on any other terms? The very question, coming from the Saviour's lips at such a time, speaks to us of the unfathomable mystery of the atoning sacrifice of the world's Redeemer. Even then, He, passing within the edge of the storm-cloud, acknowledges the transcendent virtue of the Cross.

The silence of the Father, or it may be His whisper within, reveals to the stricken Suppliant that there is no other way. Therefore, this first petition needs no longer to be offered, for it has been already laid within the blessed Will: "Not as I will, but as Thou wilt." "The cup which the Father hath given Me," He adds, "shall I not drink it?" (John 18:11). He takes it "with a hand that trembles greatly," yet He takes it "lovingly," and will drain it to the dregs.

The prayer that now falls with insistence from His lips is a cry for strength: "O My Father, if this cannot pass away, except I drink it, Thy will be done" (Matt. 26:42). It is active obedience, not mere acquiescence, that He is learning in this storm of pain. He prays that He may be enabled *to do* the will of His Father; to this end He pleads that He may be saved out of death. He is in the throes of an appalling conflict, where death, the last enemy, now reinforced by the prince of evil himself, is contending with Him for the mastery. Our Redeemer's spirit and soul are unshaken, but His physical force is weakened in the greatness of His way. To human sensitiveness it might appear as if He must fail in the hour of battle, as if His alliance with our manhood would force Him to renounce the due reward of His pain and toil. "Thy will *be done*," He prayed; He passionately craved that He might be enabled to perform it—"And there appeared unto Him an angel from heaven, strengthening Him. And being in an agony, He prayed more earnestly: and His sweat became as it were great drops of blood falling down upon the ground" (Luke 22:43-44).

Poets and painters have endeavoured to depict the manner in which this succouring angel conveyed the comfort of God. It has been suggested by one that the angel brought a personal word of encouragement from the Father; by another, that he reminded our Saviour of the provisions of the covenant enacted before time began; by a third, that he disclosed the significance of the atoning death; another represents the angel as striking the harp of God and sounding forth the anthem of those who stand by the shores of the crystal sea redeemed, of those who worship the Lamb that was slain. Possibly all that the angel was commissioned to do in this case, as in others (1 Kings 19:5-8; Matt. 4:11), was to renew the bodily strength of our Daysman, exhausted in the strain and travail of His mighty work of redemption. However it may have been, we can all share with Dr. John Duncan his burning desire to have intercourse in the realms of glory with "the angel who came down to strengthen My Lord in His agony in the garden." "I have a wonderful affection," he would say, "for that angel."

For the second time our Saviour rises from His agony of prayer, to bend over the slumbering forms of His disciples (Matt. 26:43). Perhaps nowhere else, even in the life of Jesus, can we discover a nobler example of love forgetting its own great need in solicitude for the welfare of others.

Backward and forward thrice He ran, not so much to be solaced by human sympathy, though it had been a comfort to Him to know that these beloved ones were near when His agony befell, as to bring to them the succour of God wherewith He Himself had been sustained. Then He returned and flung Himself again upon the trampled grass, saying the same words: "O My Father, if this cannot pass away, except I drink it, Thy will be done." Ere long the victory was given; the powers of hell were broken, the dragon of the pit was crushed under the Redeemer's conquering heel. "Oh my soul," He might have said with the Hebrew prophetess, "thou hast trodden down strength" (Judges 5:21).

Returning to His disciples, He said to them, as a mother might, "Sleep on now, and take your rest." He knew that they were sleeping for sorrow (Luke 22:45); He understood that the flesh was weak—He Himself was touched with the feeling of their infirmity. He sat beside them, with the glory of God shining on His brow (John 18:6), until the gleam of torches in the valley below told that the betrayer was at hand. Then He roused His followers, saying: "Arise, let us be going" (Matt. 26:46)—let us go to meet them. One opportunity had passed unused, never to be recovered—they had failed to watch with Christ one hour in the Garden. The appeal to share His Gethsemane will not return: as regards this, they may sleep on and take their rest. But another field of witness is opening before them: they are now called to testify to Jesus before priests and rulers; they may even be privileged to die with Him. Gethsemane lies behind, Calvary confronts us: "Arise, let us be going."

CHAPTER 12

"Father, Forgive Them"

The ignominy of the arrest, the trials, and evil-questionings are over. The cross-beam is laid on shoulders bruised and torn with the leaded scourge, and the Sufferer goes forth bearing His reproach. Weakened with pain, He sinks under the load. Simon of Cyrene, coming up at that moment, is impressed to share the grim burden. So the sad procession comes to Golgotha.

The cross-beam was probably laid on the ground, and our Lord stretched upon it. The nails were driven through His hands, and an iron spike pierced His feet. In the blinding agony that followed, instead of the maniacal curses the Roman soldiers were accustomed to hear on such occasions, the tender tones of the Blessed One, supplicating pardon for His murderers, fell on their ears. Well might the centurion bear witness, "Certainly, this was a righteous man. Truly this was a Son of God" (Luke 23:47; Matt. 27:54).

"Father"—this is the first word uttered from the Cross (Luke 23:34). Our Lord is going into a darkness deeper than human despair, into a desolation which none of His people can ever know; but He goes trustfully, relying securely on that name on which Jehovah had caused Him to hope. He advances to meet the doom of our sin as a loving child will hasten to greet His father, who comes to reward and bless. "I am not alone," He is able still to say, "the Father is with Me."

The immediate reference of this prayer is to the soldiers, the unquestioning instruments of Roman justice. Truly, they knew not what they did. In all likelihood they had no knowledge of the career of the prophet of Galilee, nor had they watched the course of the trial, endeavouring to sift truth from falsehood. This was to them an ordinary malefactor, condemned by the processes of law to expiate His crimes upon the Cross. "Father, forgive them," prayed our Master; "they know not what they do."

May we widen the reference, taking it as inclusive of the Jewish nation, its rulers and the body of the people? Simon Peter, in Solomon's porch, may have had this prayer in his mind when he addressed in these terms the worshippers clustering round: "Ye denied the Holy and Righteous One, and asked for a murderer to be granted unto you. . . . and now, brethren, I wot that in ignorance ye did it, as did also your rulers" (Acts 3:14,17). It is hard to think that Annas and Caiaphas, and others of their faction, did not possess an inward conviction that Jesus was all that He professed to be. The rulers seem to have known that this was the very Christ. Yet the enormity of their guilt in compassing His death was hidden from them: they were able to understand only in the most fragmentary way all that their action involved. And the love of Jesus finds in this an argument for the bestowal on them of the riches of grace. No sinner is able in this life fully to comprehend the significance of his own iniquity. Would he be able to commit sin if he did? Can any one who is not a devil deliberately say, "Evil, be thou my good"?

In this view, therefore, the prayer of Jesus reaches out to all mankind. His requests for His own are within His covenant of priesthood, and are infallibly granted. This (if we may make the distinction) is the supplication of One who was in all things like unto ourselves, who breathes out love and pity even under the strokes of the hammer and the first overwhelming sharpness of the Cross. We cannot draw from it the conclusion that all men shall be eternally saved: but in this supplication of the Lamb of God we learn to pray. We not only forgive those who may have injured us, we unfeignedly desire that they shall receive the pardoning grace of God.

This prayer of the dying Lord was harmonious with the course of His life; and we have His constant example to guide us in our prayers for pardon to those who have done us wrong: "For hereunto you were called: because Christ also suffered for you, leaving you an example, that ye should follow His steps: who did no sin, neither was guile found in His mouth: who, when He was reviled, reviled not again; when He suffered, threatened not; but committed Himself to Him that judgeth righteously" (1 Pet. 2:21-23). We should always cherish a spirit of love and forgiveness, being ready at any moment to let that mind of charity express itself in word or act of mercy. St. Paul exhorts the Colossian believers to "put on Christ," and he draws out the particulars of that sacred investiture thus: "Put on therefore, as God's elect, holy and beloved, a heart of compassion, kindness, humbleness of mind, meekness, long-suffering; forbearing one another, and forgiving each other, if any man have a complaint against any; even as the Lord forgave you, so also do ye" (Col. 3:12-13).

It is most fitting that we should add in our own case the palliative our Lord offered with regard to the soldiers: "they know not what they do." For any offence against us is not a clear contravention of justice. There is in us so much to justify any hostile judgment on the part of those who are not well-affected toward us. Our character is tarnished with defects of various kinds, which mitigate the severity of the offence committed against us; and in the very article in which we protest against blame, we are found open in measure to hostile criticism. If those who impugn us had a clearer vision they would discern much that is now hidden from their eyes, and their bitter estimate would be softened. They would be able to discount our shortcomings, and appraise with a just valuation our efforts to live worthily. In the meantime, let us commit ourselves to Him that judgeth righteously, and if any one shall have wrought us evil, let us pray, "Father, forgive them."

It is the dying Christ who asks the Father to grant forgiveness to those who crucify Him and put Him to an open shame. It is in the death of our Lord Jesus that forgiveness comes from God to sinners of Adam's race. It is His blood that cleanseth us from all sin.

> Do Thou with hyssop sprinkle me,
> I shall be cleansed so;
> Yea, wash Thou me, and then I shall
> Be whiter than the snow.

CHAPTER 13

"Why Hast Thou Forsaken Me?"

Our Lord has made intercession for His murderers (Luke 23:34), has rescued from the second death the soul of the penitent robber (Luke 23:39-43), has commended His mother to the care of the beloved disciple (John 19:25-27); now He enters on this last dread conflict. Darkness falls upon the cross, veiling the agonies of the Sufferer from unsympathetic eyes. And the Father hides His face from the Son; it pleased the Lord to bruise Him; He hath put Him to grief (Isa. 53:10).

Immanuel, the bearer of our sins, has entered the presence of the All-holy, and stands, as it were, before the Judgment Throne. He who knew no sin was made sin for us (2 Cor. 5:21). He carries our sinfulness into the light of Jehovah's countenance, taking our guilt upon Himself and making the turpitude of our sin His own. The divine lightnings smite the Sufferer; an end is made of sin and the transgression is finished. And Jesus cries, "My God, My God, why hast Thou forsaken Me?" (Matt. 27:46). God cannot look upon sin, and our Lord has assumed our iniquity in so far as it was possible for Him to do this without personal culpability.

This cry of desolation is the opening prayer of Psalm 22. It is, no doubt, the poignant experience of a suffering saint of the olden time. It is possible that David, climbing the slopes of Olivet with dust-covered head and unsandalled feet, fleeing from his unnatural son and his rebellious subjects, uncrowned, dethroned, and fugitive (2 Sam. 15), may have first uttered this bitter lament. But as his meditations ran clear, the Psalmist saw in his own grief the foreshadowing of a more appalling distress; he found himself walking in the appointed path of the Messiah.

It has been suggested by some expositors that the Lord Jesus may have rehearsed in spirit the verses of this Psalm, and that its closing words—"He hath done it" (v. 31)—may have given form to the Saviour's shout of triumph—"It is finished" (John 19:30).

The Psalmist first encourages himself in God, the Holy One, who is the very truth, and cannot deny Himself. Afterward he reaffirms his lifelong confidence in him who is the worship of his Israel. On this twofold ground of assurance he poises his prayer, which beats up through the darkness into the presence of the Eternal. In the crisis of his agony, a fore-gleam of morning shoots through the shroud of night. "Yea, from the horns of the wild oxen—Thou hast answered me" (v. 21). From this time the Psalm wings its way into the unshadowed light.

"Why hast Thou forsaken Me?' We may take this interrogation in two ways. First, as a challenge to the divine righteousness. Why should He who knew no sin be smitten? Why should this One whose faith had never faltered be permitted to die in darkness? Why should the Son, who always did the things which pleased the Father, be forsaken in His direst need? The very prayer gives a verdict. There must be a victorious issue for such a one out from among the snares of death, the pains of hell. The cloud will break, and the eternal glory shine through.

Or we may take it thus. There was in our Lord's mind, even when He was enduring the wrath of God due to us for sin, a sense of mystery. As Son of Man, feeling and thinking under conditions suitable to our manhood, the meaning of the vicarious sacrifice may, in that hour of utter darkness, have seemed to Him not wholly clear. For the atonement is the revelation of all the mysteries which surround us. It sends its piercing light into the recesses of the divine nature, and it illumines the deep places of the human spirit.

Or, it may be, this cry has a retrospective force, as if we should translate it, "My God, My God, why didst Thou forsake Me?" The darkness is passing, the cloud of dereliction melts into the light of heaven, the battle with principalities and powers is ended. And just before the exceeding great cry, "It is finished," goes ringing through earth and heaven and hell, our Saviour turns in love to His Father to ask, "Why didst Thou forsake Me?"

It is noticeable, however, that in the midnight of His pain our Lord does not employ the word "Father." He has done so before; He will do so again. But in this moment the sweetness of the Father's love has been withdrawn. And Jesus rests on the covenant—the covenant of eternity, ordered in all things and sure. "My God, My God, why hast THOU forsaken Me?" Feelings may ebb with the tides, but the rock unshaken remains, the eternal truth, the faithfulness of God. It is firm as Jehovah's throne, it is steadfast as His Name. The faith of our Redeemer is vindicated, and now He declares in words which He had taken up into His High-Priestly Prayer:

I will declare Thy name unto My brethren:
In the midst of the congregation will I praise Thee.
(Ps. 22:22; Heb. 2:12)

The dying Christ goes back, as men so often do in the hour and article of death, to the days of His childhood. Aramaic was His mother-tongue, the vernacular of Galilee of the Gentiles. It was in that speech that His mother first recounted to Him the wonderful works of God; it was the language of His boyhood and youth; and it is in that dialect that He utters His dying appeal to the God of the old time.

Speaking after the manner of men, may we not say that there was an edge of remonstrance in this prayer? God, however, permits His people to take liberties with Him. Asaph, stung with the injustice which he sees on every hand, declares, "Verily, I have cleansed my heart in vain" (Ps. 73:13). "Why art Thou so far from me, O my God?" complains another afflicted saint. Another enters this resolution upon his tablets: "I will say unto God my rock, why hast thou forgotten me?" (Ps. 42:9). Many others bring their complaints and challenges to the foot of the Throne; and God is willing to have it so, if they come before the righteous Judge with reverent faith, to supplicate justice.

Almost the next word which Jesus utters is the sacred Name "Father" (Luke 23:46). The sin of mankind no longer veils the face of Love from the suffering Son. And now, listen!

"IT IS FINISHED!"

CHAPTER 14

*"Into Thy Hands
I Commend My Spirit"*

"And when Jesus had cried with a loud voice, He said, Father, into Thy hands I commend My Spirit: and having said this He gave up the ghost" (Luke 23:46).

After the tense silence that held the watchers round the Cross had been broken by the shout of victory, our Lord surrendered His life as a sacrificial offering to God. The darkness of forsakenness has passed. The comfort of the Father's presence in love and power has been renewed, and faith returns to the joy of full assurance. The prayer which was the instrument of the dismissal of the soul of Jesus from the body of His humiliation was in its original use a cry of distress on the part of one who, "worn out in mind and body, despised, defamed, and persecuted . . . casts himself upon God" (Ps. 31:5). There are, however, two points of difference between its application to the need of the Psalmist and its employment by the dying Christ: the Psalmist invokes the name of Jehovah, God of the Covenant, and adds to His prayer this argument: "Thou hast redeemed Me" (Ps. 31:5). Jesus calls upon His Father, and dies on the merit of His own work of redemption.

In the Psalter these words are found in connection, not with the laying down of life, but with the distresses and deliverances of this mortal life. We may be sure that our Lord often applied them to this current use before He appropriated them to be the watchword of His passage from earth to the skies. As He was about to die, so He had lived, committing Himself in every hour of trial to the loving care of His Father in heaven. It was, therefore, most natural that He should quote this formula in the article of death.

"Father," the first recorded utterance of Jesus (Luke 2:29), and the last, is the sum of the disclosure of the Divine Name which the Saviour came to earth to declare: it is the revelation of Jesus Christ which God gave unto Him, to show unto His servants. God is the Father of our Lord Jesus Christ, and, by the grace of the Incarnation, our Father in Him. Faith has won its perfect triumph in the utterance of those faltering words. The Man of Sorrows and the Acquainted with Grief, with the dew of Gethsemane's agony upon His brow and the sin of a lost world upon His soul, lays His bruised but victorious life in the hands of infinite love and measureless power, the hands of His Father. Herein is faith made perfect.

May we not see in these words also an assertion of the voluntariness of our Redeemer's death? He is not overborne in dying, forced by a mightier hand into the dust of death. He lays His life down of Himself, no man taking it from Him (John 10:18). He submits to death, not because He is under constraint to obey its behests, but because He has come to do His Father's will: "This commandment," He says, "received I from My Father." To Him death was not a return to kindred dust, but an entrance into the Father's house. In His eventful journey, by water and by blood, the Redeemer of men has now reached the golden gates: the Father comes forth to welcome Him. "Now come I to Thee," He says (John 17:13), and in the power of His own blood He enters the everlasting habitations. Our Saviour does not propose to hasten His own departure, nor will He suffer His life to be taken from the earth by hostile powers; dying, He places His soul with unshaken confidence within the clasp of His Father's sheltering hand.

These words tell us that the redemptive work of the Saviour is completed. The mightiest work ever engaged in on this earth was undertaken in the name of the Holy Trinity by the Incarnate Son. He came to reconcile the world to God, to effect an agreement in a disordered creation between mercy and truth, to accomplish the salvation of the lost, to break the tyranny of evil powers, to despoil sin of its unrighteous dominion, to procure for the ungodly the ministration of the Holy Spirit, and to open the doors of His Father's house to wanderers returning from the land of famine. In bringing these things to pass He endured to the uttermost the sorrows of our mortal state, the contradiction of sinners against Himself, the stroke of God's afflictive justice. And now "it is finished": His travail and His toil are ended.

'Tis finished—was His latest voice;
These sacred accents o'er,
He bowed His head, gave up the ghost,
And suffered pain no more.

'Tis finished—the Messiah dies
For sins, but not His own;
The great redemption is complete,
And Satan's power o'erthrown.

Therefore we may pray, as the Psalmist did many centuries ago. When the sorrows of death compass us and the pains of hell lay hold upon us; when our sins, like a pack of wolves, are in full cry after our soul; then may we flee unto God our refuge, saying, "Into thine hand I commend my spirit: Thou hast redeemed me, O Lord, Thou God of truth" (Ps. 31:5).

In this last prayer of His earthly life our Lord has taught us how to die. In all generations the cry of the departing Saviour has rung out as a challenge before the everlasting doors. "The many instances on record," says one, "including St. Polycarp, St. Basil, Epiphanius of Pavia, St. Bernard, St. Louis, Huss, Columbus, Luther, and Melanchthon—of Christians using these words at the approach of death, represent many millions of unrecorded cases." The Lord gave the word; great was the company of those who published it.

Was there not also in this prayer of the departing Christ an announcement of His ascent from humiliation to exaltation? He dismissed His spirit; it took its flight to the shelter of the eternal love, the radiance of the unshadowed glory; henceforth it dwells, far from the distances and darkness of this earthly life in the Bosom of God. At times our Lord had seemed to anticipate this hour with intense longing: "O faithless and perverse generation, how long shall I be with you, and suffer you?" (Luke 9:41). "I came to cast fire upon the earth, and what will I, if it is already kindled? But I have a baptism to be baptized with; and how am I straitened till it be accomplished" (Luke 12:49-50). "And now I am no more in the world, but these are in the world, and I come to Thee" (John 17:11). The Man of Sorrows is anointed with the oil of gladness above His fellows (Heb. 1:9), the Pilgrim Christ re-enters His Father's house, the Lamb that was slain is seated in the midst of the throne, crowned with that radiancy of love which was His before the foundation of the world.

Chapter 15

"He Ever Liveth to Make Intercession"

When the forty days of our Lord's risen life on earth were ended, "He led them out until they were over against Bethany: and He lifted up His hands, and blessed them. And it came to pass, while He blessed them, He parted from them, and was carried up into heaven" (Luke 24:50-51). This farewell benediction was the signal of the Redeemer's entrance on His ministry of intercession: the nail-pierced hands, lifted over the bowed heads of the disciples, are to us the symbol of His unchangeable priesthood, and the assurance that He ever liveth to make intercession for us (Heb. 7:25).

The heavenly ministry of Christ was foreshadowed in His High-Priestly Prayer. The words "I pray" do not imply entreaty, but a request as between equals, and this idea is strengthened by the use of the phrase "I will" (see John 17:9, 15, 20, 24). Our Lord is no longer the lowly suppliant of earth, wearing the servant's girdle, and perfecting His obedience even unto death (Phil. 2:7-8), but the Man who is Jehovah's Fellow. He intercedes from the throne; He offers His requests in the power of an accepted sacrifice; He asks for that purchased possession which is His by right.

It is in the office of Mediator that the Lord Jesus presents His petitions to the Father. "There is one God, one Mediator also between God and men, Christ Jesus, Himself man" (1 Tim. 2:5). To this high function the

Messiah has been appointed of old in the eternal covenant. It is His place to make reconciliation between a righteous Judge and sinners of mankind; it is His right to redeem. St. John, with the piercing theological insight which characterises his First Epistle, sets forth this mediatorial ministry in all its fullness: "We have an Advocate with the Father, Jesus Christ the righteous: and He is the propitiation for our sins; and not for ours only, but also for the whole world" (1 John 2:1-2). Our Saviour mediates on the ground of His finished work—because He has expiated our sins; nay, more, because He is the Expiator, bearing in wounded hands and feet, and brow, and side the assurance that all which could hinder our approach to God has been taken away. It is in the power of His blood that He pleads. And justice is, in Him, and for His sake, so strongly enlisted in our favour and defence, that "Jesus Christ the Righteous" presents the claim of His own righteousness in such wise that it shall have authority with "the Father" confirming and energising the tender love of Him who gave His Son to the death on our behalf.

And how willing that Father is to respond to the righteous plea of the Well-beloved, a saying of the Lord Jesus Himself makes manifest: "In that day ye shall ask in My name: and I say not unto you, that I will make request of the Father for you; for the Father Himself loveth you" (John 16:26-27). Our prayers, ascending in the name of the Lord Jesus, are taken up into His intercession, being presented by Him before the throne, with all authority, as if the prayers were His alone; but, says He, there is more than this. It is not only that I shall make intercession for you, precious as that assurance is, but the Father's love is already eagerly anticipating those requests, that He may fulfil all your desires and bestow upon you every good and perfect gift: "The Father Himself loveth you." And it is of this that the Saviour would have His people think, even more than of His advocacy for them. Few things could pain our Master more than that, in remembering Him, we should forget the Father who is the Fountain of Godhead love.

It would be idle to ask what form this heavenly advocacy assumes. The writer of the Epistle to the Hebrews passes beyond all forms to the undying essence: "For Christ entered not into a holy place made with hands, like in pattern to the true; but into heaven itself, now to appear before the face of God for us" (Heb. 9:24). Our High Priest, having offered Himself, now presents Himself in the power of a risen life before God on our behalf. As He Himself is the propitiation, so He Himself is the availing intercession. St. John has put this thought into glowing imagery. When the challenge of the strong angel sounded through earth and heaven, "Who is worthy to open the book, and to loose the seals thereof?" a Lamb, as it had been slain—our Lord, coming up from the conflict and agony of His passion—advanced to the throne, and took the book of the world's guidance out of the hand of Him that liveth for ever and ever. Then all the choirs of heaven raised the new song of victorious love: "Thou art worthy to take the book, and to open the seals thereof: for Thou was slain, and didst purchase unto God with Thy blood men of every tribe and tongue, and people, and nation" (Rev. 5:1-10).

It is in the Epistle to the Hebrews that our Lord's heavenly ministry is most clearly set forth. A verse which throws a flood of light upon the importance of this priestly action of the risen Lord is, "He, because He abideth for ever, hath His priesthood unchangeable. Wherefore also He is able to save to the uttermost them that draw near unto God through Him, seeing He ever liveth to make intercession for them" (Heb. 7:24-25). He lives to intercede. This is the sum of all His priestly activities in the heavens. From His intercession flow the donation of the Spirit and the ministration of spiritual gifts, the growth of grace in the lives of the redeemed, and all the sanctifying influences which proceed from the Father's providential care and the mediatorial ministry of the Redeemer.

Let us mention one or two of the fruits of our Saviour's intercession.

(a) It secures to us peace of conscience, and the assurance of the Father's free and unalterable forgiveness: "Who is He that shall condemn? It is Christ that died, yea rather, that was raised from the dead, who is at the right hand of God, who also maketh intercession for us" (Rom. 8:34).

(b) It provides for our complete sanctification. In a text already quoted we read, "He is able to save to the uttermost"—this in the power of His intercession. Not only *from the uttermost*—that, thank God, He is able to do—but *to the uttermost*, piercing to the thoughts and intents of the heart, reaching to the springs of feeling and desire, and presenting us faultless before the Father.

(c) In several passages in the Old Testament the Messiah is represented as leading the worship of Israel. Our Lord seems to accept this view of His heavenly ministry, as when He says, "Where two or three are gathered together in My name, there am I in the midst of them" (Matt. 18:20). One may well believe that our Lord in His intercession is continually ministering grace through all the ordinances of the Church.

In a word, the exalted Saviour is fulfilling the command of His Father: "Ask of Me, and I will give Thee the nations for Thine inheritance, and the uttermost parts of the earth for Thy possession" (Ps. 2:8). He is praying, as He has taught us to pray, for the coming of that time when the kingdoms of this world shall become the Kingdom of our Lord and of His Christ, when Jehovah shall be Ruler over all the earth, when there shall be one Lord, and His Name one. From henceforth He is "expecting" until all shall do Him reverence.

GRANTED
MINISTRIES
— PRESS —

WHAT YOU CAN AFFORD POLICY

As with all of the resources that we make available, this book is offered to any who believe they can benefit from it, whether they can pay for it or not. There is a cost for the book, but we do not want this to be an obstacle to anyone. If you cannot afford to purchase a copy, or if you can only afford a portion of the price, we ask that you write and give us the opportunity to serve God by providing for His people. Our only stipulation is that you not request the book unless you are certain to read it within six months. We do not want to generously enlarge your library, but to generously enlarge your spiritual condition.

GRANTED MINISTRIES PRESS
120 N. Third St.
Hannibal, MO 63401
www.grantedministries.org

That in all things He might have preeminence

Granted Ministries strives to make the very best Christian teaching available around the world. We do this primarily through our website and also through the printing of books and distribution of discs. We are a non-profit charity seeking to serve Christ faithfully by diligently helping His church to know Him more fully.

www.grantedministries.org

CLEAR ADVICE

EASY NAVIGATION

MINISTRY PRICES

TRUSTED CONTENT.